SAIGON COOKBOOK

VIETNAMESE CUISINE AND CULTURE
IN SOUTHERN CALIFORNIA'S LITTLE SAIGON

Ann Le

With photographs by Julie Fay Ashborn

SECOND EDITION

Guilford, Connecticut

Project editor: David Legere
Text design: Nancy Freeborn
Maps by Multimapping Ltd. © Morris Book Publishing, LLC.
Photo credits: pp. viii, xi, and 96 courtesy Ann Le; pp. 145 and 163 photos.com. All others © Julie Fay
Ashborn.

The Library of Congress has cataloged the earlier edition as follows:
Le, Ann.
    The little Saigon cookbook : Vietnamese cuisine and culture in Southern California's
little Saigon / Ann Le. — 1st ed.
      p. cm.
    Includes index.
    ISBN 0-7627-3831-6
1. Cookery, Vietnamese. I. Title.
    TX724.5.V5L42 2006
    641.59597—dc22

2005024893

Printed in China
10 9 8 7 6 5 4 3 2 1

This book is dedicated to bà ngoại, Phu Dang.

For Mom, Bobo, Kim, and our family, and the people of Little Saigon.

Contents

Acknowledgments

This book would not have been possible without the efforts, support, and existence of the following:

My editors, Cary Hull and Laura Strom. Cary's the one who wrote the book. Thanks for telling me to try a little harder every time. You made it easy. Laura, thanks for your faith and support, and for simply being a wonderful person who happens to also be my editor.

The folks at Globe Pequot Press for teaching me so much.

Julie Fay, for the beautiful photography in this book. You are such a pleasure to work with.

Kim Fay, for supporting this book and everything Vietnamese.

Ong Du Mien, Professor Jeffrey Brody, and Derrick Nguyen, for sharing your stories, insights, and research. The community is lucky to have you as its participants and leaders.

Daniel Medina, for editing, proposal work, all kinds of support and hand-holding.

Johanna Wilkie, Tony Cronin, and Wesley Medina, for extra editing help, and especially Johanna for helping me clean up after those wild, hedonistic recipe-testing parties.

Cecilia De Robertis for editing, proposal help, and cheerleading.

Maya Lee, for top-notch professional and legal advice and friendship.

Astute recipe testers and contributors to the cookbook suggestion box: Dan, Lika, Twiggy, Johanna, Courtney, Cindy, Benjamin, Marianne and the Sanbongi family, Jules, Adam and Lynn, Aaron, Kayron, Cousin Long, Cousin Yen, Brother

Kim, Yumna, Brittany, Brynn, Ken, Cousin Kathy, Mandy Kahn, Kramer, Maya, Sammy P., Lenora, Gabe, Ben Nicolas, and—last but not least—Irene Ribner. Thank you for your eating and for your friendships.

Norman Kolpas, for your generous help with my proposal and the introduction to the biz.

A million thanks for the cooperation and help from the establishments and people in Little Saigon, especially Chua Hue Quang, Thu Vien Vietnam, My Nguyen, Trieu Chau, Banh Mi Che Cali, and Pho Tau Bay.

I'm always grateful for my loving family, and in this case for recipes, support, and heartfelt stories.

And finally, thank you to the wonderful people of Little Saigon. The community and the people who make it up all serve as my inspiration.

During *vuot bien,* my family split into two different boats. Here are my grandparents with just half of my family in Minneapolis, Minnesota, in 1975.

Introduction

There's a rule followed by savvy diners looking for the ultimate in ethnic authenticity: *Eat where the locals eat*. The search for authentic Vietnamese food in the United States will always end in one community, Little Saigon, in Southern California's Orange County. Here lies a spectacular enclave, built by extraordinary immigrants who started with virtually nothing. Today, in an area of roughly 3 square miles, Little Saigon is home to more than 4,000 Vietnamese American businesses and 200 restaurants—and the largest population of Vietnamese outside Vietnam.

Located fifteen minutes southwest of Disneyland and forty-five minutes southeast of downtown Los Angeles, Little Saigon is one of Orange County's most exotic tourist attractions. People come from many miles around to this remarkable self-contained community to visit its Buddhist temples, its beautiful parks and historical monuments, and its one-of-a-kind shops selling jewelry, herbal medicines, and much more. But they also come—in droves—for the fabulous Vietnamese food served or sold at mom-and-pop restaurants, specialty bakeries, pho houses, sandwich delis, supermarkets, coffeehouses, and banquet-style restaurants.

For locals such as me and my family, all the bustle of Little Saigon is simply our everyday world. But beneath the commerce and commotion lies a deeper reality that visitors to our enclave may not immediately see: The shops and eateries here have for years sustained their immigrant population nutritionally, emotionally, even spiritually. There is a history and rich culture to Little Saigon. And it's the cuisine that ties it all together.

I wrote this book to preserve the recipes that the Vietnamese people—among them my own relatives—brought with us when we left Vietnam for the shores of our new homeland, America. I love my heritage, I love my family, I love Little Saigon, and, of course, I love the food that is so inextricably part of my world.

A BRIEF HISTORY OF LITTLE SAIGON

Not just another ethnic community, Little Saigon is an evolving culture and a living, breathing symbol of survival.

Between 1975 and 2000 more than two million Vietnamese fled their homeland. The first two waves of mass emigration are known as *vuot biên* (translated as "to flee by sea"). My parents, grandparents, and aunts and uncles were among those who escaped Vietnam as boat people, leaving their homes just three days before the fall of Saigon in April 1975. Their escape was fueled by rumors of a Communist-led bloodbath.

Many of the South Vietnamese who remained in Vietnam after 1975 were sent to what the Hanoi government referred to as "reeducation camps." The stories of those who survived these camps and are now living in the United States are being collected and archived within Little Saigon. According to their accounts, these prisoners were subjected to hard labor, given little to eat, sometimes tortured or killed. Many risked their lives to flee Vietnam by boat in another *vuot biên* that continued throughout the 1980s.

Archives and information on the reeducation camp experience can be found at the University of California–Irvine's Southeast Asian Archive. Another organization, Boat People SOS, has been actively working with Vietnamese Americans to chronicle the stories of reeducation camp survivors, and to bring their experiences to the attention of the media and the government.

Once at sea, the refugees continued to suffer great hardship. Many left behind not only homes and possessions but also loved ones. Most found themselves in overcrowded wooden fishing and shrimp boats. Only the fortunate were picked up by larger boats; it is believed that more than half of the boat people died at sea.

Those who made it across the sea alive were settled in refugee camps across Asia, but these nations were unwilling to allow the refugees citizenship. President Gerald Ford then oversaw the passage of the Indochina Migration and Refugee Act of 1975, and the United States began airlifting refugees from camps all over Asia onto American soil. Literally overnight, military bases throughout the country became refugee camps. One of these was Camp Pendleton in Southern California, whose warm, sunny coastal climate reminded many Vietnamese of their lost homeland.

My grandma and her three daughters in Canh Tho, Vietnam, 1952.

In the 1970s Orange County, California, largely consisted of suburban, Caucasian, middle-class neighborhoods; it also had abundant farmland. The cities of Westminster and Garden Grove—both close to Camp Pendleton—weren't sharing in the otherwise widespread abundance, however. Many longtime residents had

been forced to seek work elsewhere, leaving behind their homes, farms, and businesses. In 1979 commercial rents in these areas were only thirty-five cents per square foot. (Today, by contrast, they're thirty-five *dollars* per square foot!)

As the Vietnamese refugees began to leave Camp Pendleton to take up their new lives, most stayed in the area they'd come to enjoy. All of them, however, had to deal with severe time and money constraints when it came to feeding themselves and their families. With limited English skills and no American job skills or training, options were few.

Yet one thing almost all of the former boat people could do was cook. With cheap real estate available in Westminster and Garden Grove—especially the storefronts along the Bolsa Avenue strip—the idea of opening up a restaurant became viable for many. Some of the very first "restaurants" were set up in the dining room of a cook's own home. These simple restaurants eventually became places where friends and neighbors who were working long hours could find inexpensive, home-cooked meals.

The name *Little Saigon,* of course, honors the former capital of South Vietnam. After the war, Saigon was renamed Ho Chi Minh City. Calling their adopted California community "Little Saigon" is one way that Vietnamese refugees keep the old Saigon of Vietnam alive in their hearts. Indeed, some half dozen commemorative events are held each year on April 30— the anniversary of Saigon's fall.

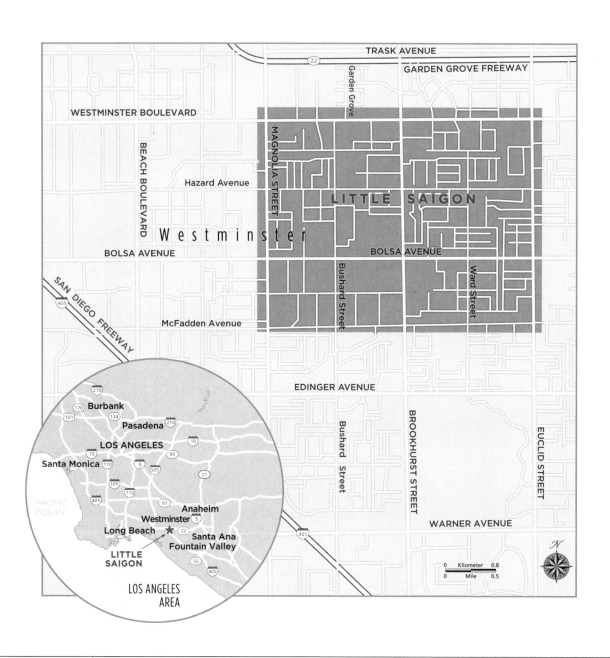

I was one of these diners. My parents used to work until eight thirty every night at their business in the community, and it was cheaper for our family to eat at restaurants around Little Saigon than it would have been to buy groceries and cook at home. So we patronized our neighborhood eateries, ordering spring rolls, egg rolls, simple rice dishes with grilled meat, noodle salads, and porridges. Not only did these comfort dishes help meet our cravings for home, but they also provided a simple, well-balanced meal for those of us pinching pennies.

It did not take many years before those Vietnamese refugees who concentrated in Westminster and Garden Grove developed the area into the dynamic enclave we see today. In June 1988, California Governor Deukmejian officially designated the area of Bolsa Avenue between Ward and Magnolia Avenues as "Little Saigon."

A PORTRAIT OF LITTLE SAIGON

The Vietnamese community has thrived in America, and with it Little Saigon has expanded as far as the 22 Freeway to the north, the 405 Freeway to the south, Beach Boulevard on the west, and Harbor Boulevard on the east. Yet little 3-mile Bolsa Avenue, the birthplace of our neighborhood, remains its heart, soul—and, of course, stomach!

If you come to visit Little Saigon, you will be surrounded everywhere along this avenue by the sights, sounds, smells, and tastes of Vietnam—and the lively culture of the Vietnamese. You'll see long lines of laughing, talking shoppers snaking out the doors of fresh food markets. Twenty-five- and fifty-pound bags of jasmine rice line the front doorways, while cell phones and lottery tickets are sold next to them in designated booths. Vietnamese pop music blares throughout the stores. Just a few feet farther down the street, you can join the throng at a pho house, where you may find yourself sharing a table with complete strangers. Soup and an appropriate salad platter will be brought to you within minutes of ordering. At these and most Little Saigon restaurants, you'll eat with plasticware; nap-

kins are distributed from a dispenser, and the furnishings and cookware are old and well worn. Things can seem cluttered. All of this may strike visitors as a bit lowbrow, but there is undeniable charm and character here as well.

Spiritual life in the form of Buddhism and Catholicism pervades our enclave. More than fifty Buddhist houses of worship dot Little Saigon, many of them simply ranch houses transformed through prayer and statuary; others are magnificent temples. Weekend worship and activity are never solemn or quiet. Churches, temples, and shrines along Bolsa Avenue all bustle with commotion and laughter.

Continue down the street and you can peek into a banquet restaurant where families and friends find any excuse to celebrate with food. Tables are traditionally round; with no one sitting at head or foot, there is no pride of place here. A lazy Susan in the middle of each table ensures equal access to the feast. Outside, fishmongers sell seafood only minutes away from the ocean. Bakeries and coffeehouses serve as centers of sustenance, community, and sweet treats with a Vietnamese twist.

What you'll *rarely* see on the streets of Little Saigon are Vietnamese people on their own, without a friend or even stranger to talk to. The Vietnamese move in packs; it is part of our culture to take pictures together, eat together, do everything together. If someone is ever alone, she is deep in contemplation, or reading a book or the newspaper. And she isn't alone for long.

LITTLE SAIGON CUISINE

Bona fide Vietnamese food—the kind you can always count on finding in Little Saigon—is simple and traditional, yet it also satisfies the adventurous food lover. It is characterized by a balance of understated flavors emphasizing freshness, while its uniqueness lies in its essential ingredients—above all, fish sauce and fresh herbs and vegetables. Vietnamese flavors are deep, yet subtle and not as heavy and rich as Thai or Indian foods. The cuisine is known for its delicate and healthful dishes, many of which are vegetarian. There is a healthy reliance on steamed rice, and steaming in general is very popular. Meat and fish are not often considered main courses, but simply one part of the family's evening meal. Vietnamese food uses

little oil; we prefer to sauté foods in their own juices rather than adding more oil. Even dipping sauces and salad dressings are citrus-based.

Looked at as a whole, the Vietnamese table is a conglomeration of Vietnam's three regional cuisines. Vietnam is separated geographically into three distinct areas: the North, the Central, and the South, with Hanoi, Hue, and Saigon (now Ho Chi Minh City) as their respective major cities. Rice is the most important part of a Vietnamese meal in all three regions. North Vietnam, near China's border, has dishes influenced by the Chinese. Central Vietnam's more temperate weather, as well as significant coastlines, yields a variety of lush crops. South Vietnam, with more coastline and the Mekong River system, provides more seafood and an array of tropical foodstuffs. The majority of this book's recipes come from the South Vietnamese culinary tradition.

Many people think of Vietnamese food as French-influenced. Or Cambodian- or Chinese-influenced. It's true that Vietnam was occupied by other countries for centuries, and the results of these foreign influences are evident in Vietnamese food. However, the cuisine is not so much a conglomeration of the different influences as it is a showcase of the best of these other cuisines, including breads and pastries inspired by the French, stir-fried wok dishes from the Chinese, and curries that originated in Cambodia. All these influences—from within and without Vietnam itself—are apparent in Little Saigon, as you will see (and taste) in the chapters to come.

ABOUT THIS BOOK

The Little Saigon Cookbook is arranged in chapters that each highlight a cultural point or attraction of Little Saigon. All are based around Bolsa Avenue, the community's lifeline. Along the way, your culinary tour of Little Saigon will bring you fresh-baked treats from the bakeries; crunchy, tangy chicken and cabbage salad made from fresh ingredients found at the Asian markets; picture-perfect arrangements of vermicelli noodles with grilled lemongrass beef from the Asian Garden Mall; vegetarian delights from a Buddhist temple; perfectly braised pork in a caramel sauce served at Tet, the Vietnamese New Year; grilled beef with lemongrass and garlic from a wedding reception's lazy Susan; iced Vietnamese coffee from the local coffeehouse; and that famous meal-in-a-bowl, the pho soup served in noodle houses.

Also included is a helpful introduction to the basics of preparing Vietnamese cuisine and a thorough appendix on our traditional ingredients. Scattered throughout the book are bits of information giving you glimpses of Little Saigon and the Vietnamese culture—how traditions have evolved for Vietnamese Americans, how celebrations are held, how we shop, how we eat, and much more.

I hope this cookbook will help you create your own authentic Vietnamese dishes and learn about Little Saigon in the process. You'll find that Vietnamese culture and the people of Little Saigon are just as complex, deep, and full of life as the food and flavors you will learn to create. Little Saigon awaits your visit. It's always seventy-five degrees in Orange County, and there's always a steaming bowl of pho waiting for you.

DEMYSTIFYING VIETNAMESE FOOD

A PRIMER ON INGREDIENTS, TECHNIQUES, AND EQUIPMENT

Demystifying Vietnamese Food

A PRIMER ON INGREDIENTS, TECHNIQUES, AND EQUIPMENT

One of the great myths of Vietnamese cuisine asserts that it is impossible to make at home. And that there are so many unfamiliar names and ingredients, even a Vietnamese person would have problems with all of them. For some Americans the mere mention of Vietnamese food conjures up images of kitchen disaster. There are too many nuances to capture; how can anyone master this complex and mysterious cuisine?

But in fact, Vietnamese cuisine is usually quite simple. What makes it so lively are the assertive flavors of just a few often-used ingredients like ginger, lemongrass, scallions, chile, garlic, black pepper, fermented fish sauce, and an abundance of fresh herbs such as cilantro, Thai basil, and mint. Cooking techniques are basic, like sautéing, grilling, steaming, and light frying. What may seem complicated is in reality a simple, quick dish to prepare. The time-consuming dishes simply require patience for a hands-off, slow-cooking simmer, not hours spent searching for and preparing ingredients.

WHAT WE EAT

Food is an important part of the Vietnamese culture. It represents the time for families to be together after a busy day, and it is the principal component of celebrations and festivals. The women of the house are generally responsible for the meals, though men are expected to lend a hand, or to cook if the wife or daughter is indisposed. The quality of a woman's cooking is a reflection of her character and whether she was raised properly.

The Vietnamese pride themselves in cuisine that uses only the freshest ingredients—a principle applicable to everything from produce to seafood. Fresh herbs and vegetables play a pivotal role in the dining experience. From the citrusy, cumin-flavored rice paddy herb to the licorice and cinnamon tastes of the perilla leaf, herbs wrap a second layer of flavor around the food they adorn. Fresh produce is also important to help achieve the contrast of textures that Vietnamese cuisine is known for. Crunchy, crispy, al dente textures derived from vegetables and fruits make all the difference to otherwise simple dishes. The ubiquitous salad platter consists of sliced or julienned cucumbers, green or red leaf lettuce, bean sprouts, sprigs of mint, coriander, Thai basil, and whatever else the local garden yields.

Condiments are a defining part of Vietnamese cuisine. Dipping sauce is the most common, but some dishes call for a ginger fish sauce, peanut sauce, or a simple ginger–soy sauce combination. Condiments add a distinct, second layer to the food, creating an entirely new dimension with their pungent, umami flavor. Vietnamese food is pure, direct, and honest. But it's the condiments that add the final touch of complexity with each bite. The tastes can be so arresting that your mouth wants to hold on and study them for a while. This feeling is what Vietnamese people are most proud of in showcasing their cuisine.

Garnishes are important for taste as well as presentation. It is common to garnish a dish with some fresh herbs like mint, cilantro, or parsley, or to top off a dish with crushed peanuts, chopped scallion rings, or fried shallots or garlic. These final touches add a layer of fragrance, flavor, or texture. Whole Thai bird chiles are also added as a garnish for the sake of appearance; most people, however, can manage only a few bites of one chile at a meal.

It shouldn't be surprising that the Vietnamese, who live in a developing, Asian country, do not count carbs, or calories for that matter. If we did, 70 percent of our diet would be eliminated. Rice is the number one staple of the Vietnamese.

Steamed white rice is served at every meal. When rice isn't available, many people will use rice vermicelli as a substitute. Rice noodles, crepes, flour, and any other rice derivation are all part of our everyday consumption. Enter any Asian super-market and you'll find rice sold only in large, plastic-weave bags in five-pound increments.

With direct access to the bounty of the ocean and the Mekong River system, the Vietnamese have more than thirty varieties of fish. As a result, seafood is much more abundant in our cuisine than chicken, pork, and beef. Seafood is usu-ally grilled or steamed, but once in a while is deep-fried. Meat is served sparingly, partly because it is expensive. All meats and seafood are cooked in light, flavorful marinades, which always include fish sauce or oyster sauce. Grilled pieces of seafood and meats are wrapped in herbs, rice paper, or vegetable leaves and dipped into various sauces alongside the salad platter.

HOW WE EAT

Meals are almost always served family-style, with serving bowls in the center of the table. Diners need only chopsticks, a china rice bowl, and clean hands. With our chopsticks, we pick up bite-size portions of food, one at a time, from one of the main family dishes and place it into our rice bowl. While tipping the bowl toward our mouth, we use the chopsticks to shovel the rice and meat or vegetable in.

The Vietnamese are passionate eaters. We truly enjoy what we eat and are unrepentant about being loud eaters. It may not be proper based on Western eti-quette, but people eating loudly with their mouths slightly open, allowing aromas to circulate and enrich each bite, has never bothered me. Our food is audibly juicy. We slurp our noodles and broth and crunch into lettuce, herbs, and pickled veg-etables. We gnaw on bones and we pick tiny fish bones out of our mouths with our hands, discarding the bones into little napkins that we leave beside our rice bowls. It's all part of enjoying every bite.

THE FIFTH TASTE: UMAMI

Most of us know the four primary tastes—salty, sweet, sour, and bitter. But food technologists have long been touting Asian cuisines, specifically Vietnamese, for their ability to showcase the fifth basic taste—umami. The term *umami* was coined in the early twentieth century by a Japanese chemist who went on to invent monosodium glutamate (MSG) to enhance flavors in foods. There are those who think using MSG is the only way to increase the umami taste of a food, but that's not true.

My brother, Kim, a biochemist, describes umami simply as a breakdown of proteins. Proteins are bound together by amino acids, such as glutamate, one of the twenty most common natural amino acids. When proteins are broken down by curing, fermenting, or aging, the amino acids break down, and foods take on an entirely different flavor. Some foods created through such a process are fish sauce, soy sauce, and Parmesan cheese, and all of them have a rich umami taste. Some other foods are naturally umami-rich because of the amino acids they contain; these include ripe tomatoes, cabbage, soybeans, sweet potatoes, fish, and mushrooms.

But umami is not just about specific dishes or foods; it's about how the foods are put together. Here are some examples of how umami works to enhance flavors in Vietnamese foods:

- By adding dried mushrooms or shrimp to a pineapple dish.

- By adding fish sauce to an ordinary vegetable broth.

- By pouring a dressing made with fish sauce, lime, sugar, and chile over a cabbage salad.

- By combining tomatoes with beef in bo luc lac.

- By eating pickled shallots and garlic with grilled meats.

- By adding fermented shrimp paste to a fresh shrimp dish.

- By sprinkling dried, cured shrimp over plain rice noodle dishes or salads.

- By sautéing plain vegetables or tofu with oyster sauce.

A typical Vietnamese breakfast consists of noodle soups like pho, hu tieu, and mi, or rice congee called chao. Simple snacks are eaten as well, such as sweetened coconut milk wrapped around steamed mung beans, or savory treats wrapped in sticky rice and banana leaves. Vietnamese baguettes are eaten with a coffee or as a snack. The Vietnamese are big snackers, and from breakfast onward, fruit, nuts, che, and easy-to-grab items from a deli like banh mi thit (sandwiches) or egg rolls fill the time between meals. So do beverages, including fruit drinks, fruit shakes, teas, and soybean milk. Cafe sua da, a favorite Vietnamese coffee beverage made strong, sweet, and icy cold, is consumed mostly in the morning.

For lunch, noodle soups can still be eaten, as well as a number of other items like banh mi thit or herb noodle salads (bun) with a grilled meat or seafood topping. Turmeric rice flour crepes (banh xeo) or potato starch (banh khoai) crepes are popular, in addition to stir-fries and noodle sautés with vegetables and a little bit of meat.

The evening meal is the most important one of the day, the time when the family comes together. Generally it consists of steamed rice, a salad platter, one or two or three main dishes that include some meat and at least one seafood dish, and canh (usually a vegetable consommé that serves as the diner's beverage). The Vietnamese will sometimes serve tea before or after a meal, but no beverages are consumed during. Dessert almost always consists of fruit.

There is no prelude into the Vietnamese main meal with an appetizer course. Sometimes fried spring rolls or other hand-rolled items like goi cuon, the popular Vietnamese fresh spring rolls, will be served before a large festive meal. At a lazy Susan banquet, sometimes there is a plate of cold items, but that is generally served with a number of other dishes at the same time. You will find, however, that there are a number of Vietnamese recipes in this book that can easily become appetizers.

COOKING TOOLS

Relax. When it comes to cooking Vietnamese food, you don't need to know your way around a kitchen perfectly. But you do need to be comfortable with chopping and tasting and knowing what you like. Don't be alarmed if you taste your dishes and they don't seem salty or sweet enough. Simply adjust the spicing to your own liking. Vietnamese cooking is truly about tasting as you go—adding more salt, sugar, vegetables, herbs. This is how the art of Vietnamese cooking has been passed down from generation to generation, kitchen to kitchen.

Water is everywhere in the Vietnamese kitchen. Colanders are filled with various herbs, and lettuce and vegetables are strewn all around the sink. Vietnamese cooks are obsessed with cleaning food and rinsing it again and again. We rinse and wash produce a few times over; we make sure that seafoods and meats are completely scrubbed and cleaned. Vietnamese cooking doesn't require guts, just a whole lot of prep work.

Here are the tools you need; many of them you already have in your kitchen:

Chopsticks: Learn to use them. They are necessary for eating, but they're great for cooking with as well. There are no fast and easy rules to chopstick use; just imagine them as tweezers and keep practicing. I feel that I can toss faster and more evenly when using chopsticks for stir-fries and sautés than I can with a spatula or wooden spoon.

Clay pot: A great cooking tool and a great investment. In a covered clay pot, food can cook in minimal liquid, retaining the essential nutrients and vitamins. The ridges in the pot allow the steam and liquid to fully encircle and cook the food evenly. Clay pots are outstanding for cooking tougher cuts of meat because they help the meat stay moist and juicy. A medium-size or large unglazed clay pot is best because it can soak up considerably more water, slowing the cooking process for braising meats. Serve the food in the pot directly at the dining table, regardless of the pot's condition. Your diners will know they're having the very best of comfort foods.

Colanders: You'll need quite a few. Most will be for rinsing vegetables and herbs, but they are also necessary for draining cooked noodles, and for acting as holding bowls when you are preparing dishes that require numerous herbs and vegetables.

Cutting boards: Have two: one for meat and another for vegetables.

Food processor: This makes life a whole lot easier when you need to blend spices, but it's not always necessary if you have extra time for prep work.

Grill pan/barbecue: Many of our marinated meats and seafood are best when grilled. A simple grill pan on the stove is a great substitute when the barbecue is too much of a hassle. A grill pan also lets you retain the juices produced during the grilling process.

Knives: Julienning, chopping, coring, shredding, and such are the most time-consuming processes of prep work, so find knives that you enjoy and keep them sharp. The Asian chef knife—a cleaver with a nice thin blade—is a popular tool. My grandma uses a giant cleaver for everything.

Mandoline: Vietnamese salads (goi) and garnishes require the fine shredding and chopping of fresh vegetables. A mandoline, which resembles a cheese grater, lets you turn vegetables into paper-thin slices and tiny shreds. Prices of mandolines range widely. It is more important to find one you are comfortable with than to spend hundreds on an expensive one. An inexpensive plastic mandoline may be adequate if you don't use it often.

Mixing bowls: You need plenty to blend marinades and fish sauce condiments, as well as for simply holding vegetables and herbs.

Mortar and pestle: Great—but not fast—for crushing seeds and forming pastes as part of important rubs and marinades. If time is of the essence, a food processor can be used, but you won't get as fine a consistency.

Rice cooker: Many Vietnamese families have been using the same rice cookers for decades. I think my own is eight years old. As long as you master the art of getting the proper amount of water for perfect jasmine rice (and this will depend on each rice cooker), you'll be fine.

Saucepans: Necessary for making canh (consommé), for braising (if you don't have a clay pot), and for preparing desserts such as che. You will need medium and large sizes.

Skillet: It doesn't matter if you use a nonstick skillet or not; most Vietnamese dishes contain a little bit of oil, or the food is cooked in its own juices or a marinade.

Steamer: I bought a large, Chinese-style steamer at a great price at one of the Asian supermarkets, and it can fit a whole fish. Or you can create a makeshift steamer by placing a low rack or trivet in the center of a 12-inch skillet. Pour hot water into the skillet to just under the rack, and bring it to a boil. Place fish on an oiled, heat-resistant dish over the rack. Cover the skillet and steam for about five minutes and your fish will be ready to serve.

Stockpot: A large pot for making stock and soups. You will need an enormous one to contain all the ingredients and bones for making pho and hu tieu stocks.

Vegetable peeler: This device not only quickly peels vegetables, but also creates paper-thin shreds of root vegetables if you do not have a mandoline. It is quite advanced to someone of my grandma's generation. She can peel vegetables like carrots and taro root with—you guessed it—a cleaver.

HEAVENLY FERMENTED FISH

Fish sauce is to the Vietnamese kitchen as olive oil is to the Italian. No self-respecting Vietnamese would serve a meal without it. Combined with different ingredients, fish sauce creates many varieties of condiments essential to Vietnamese cuisine. The most popular condiment is nuoc cham (dipping sauce), made from a blend of fish sauce, lime juice, chile peppers, and sugar, and served with almost every Vietnamese dish.

The Vietnamese take the process of making fish sauce extremely seriously and view it as an art form, recognizing the importance of the quality of the fish, the salt that's used, the weather and temperature conditions, and the type of wood in the barrels used for storage. This is how fish sauce is made: Fish, generally small anchovies called ca com, are farmed from the ocean or at fish farms. They are laid out to dry over fine mesh. They are heavily salted on top. The salt dries out the fish, starting the initial fermentation process. The salt extracts liquid from the fish; this liquid drains down through the mesh into a wooden vat. The fish liquid from the vat is placed in barrels and allowed to sit longer for the breakdown of molecules to continue. The darker the fish sauce, the more fermented and the more potent.

There are more than sixty varieties of fish sauce. In Vietnamese opinion, our fish sauce is the best quality of all, surpassing Thai and Filipino sauces, simply because of Vietnam's proximity to the water and the variety of fish in the country. When shopping, look first for Vietnamese, and then for the name of the Vietnamese island of Phuc Quoc. This little island southwest of Vietnam's Mekong Delta is paradise for fish sauce lovers. A gorgeous, tropical island, it includes a large resort built by investors. The investors, however, neglected to consider that the smell of rotting fish is not a romantic fragrance, and the resort has seen very few visitors.

Phan Thiet, a small town south of Nha Trang on the coast, is also famous for its varietals of fish sauce. Fish sauce is sold in different gradations. The pungent, salty liquid is called nhì in its first extraction. Considered the finest grade in the fish sauce hierarchy, it is recommended for creating dipping sauce. Darker gradations, which resemble a thick brown sauce, are hardly ever used for cooking anymore, since the finest fish sauce is available for just a few dollars a bottle.

Fish sauce should not be applied as generously as soy sauce. There is a more complex combination of amino acids in fish than in other foods. When the proteins of fish are broken down during the fermentation process, the quality of taste is similar to that of soy sauce, beef broths, or any other umami-heavy food. Because of the high levels of amino acids—and therefore umami flavor—less fish sauce is used, but that translates to better flavors and better food.

PREPARATION TECHNIQUES

For the most part, cooking calls for some easy and basic methods, but sometimes special techniques are required. Here are a few tips on specific preparations.

Braising: An important technique that requires you to cook food slowly with a little liquid in a covered vessel, such as a clay pot or saucepan. The first step in braising is searing or browning, a crucial part of the caramelizing process in Vietnamese cuisine. You need to be patient as you prepare these slow dishes.

Caramelizing: The Vietnamese are known for kho dishes: braised, caramelized food. When sugar is cooked over medium to high heat, it will caramelize into a thick brown sauce. I like to cover meat with a generous amount of sugar before browning it, which produces a nice caramel coating. As the meat braises, the liquid and sugars will continue to cook and thicken.

Chopping: My recipe testers enjoyed the goi salads but had no idea the Vietnamese were so obsessed with chopping! I think we like chopping so much because increasing the surface area of the food makes for easier absorption of flavors and marinades. When immersed in any kind of dressing, a julienned carrot is more flavorful than an inch-long piece. Chopped, shredded, and paper-thin-sliced foods add to the presentation. Chopping is also important because all food needs to be cut into bite-size pieces for chopstick use.

Light frying: Vietnamese cuisine does not include many fried dishes, but when it does, they're never deep-fried, just lightly fried in a thin layer of oil (never lard) in a skillet or frying pan. Occasionally the food is in a light batter. The foods are generally fried for just a short amount of time and are drained immediately on paper towels. Our frying doesn't make greasy foods, but simply gives certain dishes a nice crunch.

Reconstituting: Many dried ingredients—such as shrimp and mushrooms—are important for soups, stir-fries, and braises. If a recipe calls for the reconstitution of these ingredients, save the liquid that accumulates and add it to the sauce, stir-fry, or soup you are cooking. When reconstituting any dried ingredients, use tepid water that just barely covers them, and leave them for a few hours or overnight to draw out the most flavor.

Sautéing: Requires that you cook food quickly in the right amount of oil, butter, or, in the case of Vietnamese food, a marinade, over medium to high heat. It is best to use a skillet or frying pan of a size that comfortably contains the food. The pan should be preheated. When the food is cooked quickly, it stays moist. The cooking time will vary depending on the food.

Steaming: A way to cook food without adding extra oil. It allows the food to be cooked and appreciated in its most pure form. When we steam fish, we usually do so with some sauce (fish or soy or Maggi) as well as some herbs. A dish or bowl needs to hold these contents comfortably. The fish should sit on an oiled surface or a bed of herbs to prevent it from sticking to the steamer.

THE BASICS

In every cuisine, there are always several recipes that cooks need to know: a good tomato sauce, a flour tortilla, a perfect flaky piecrust. Vietnamese cuisine also has its own list of basics—steamed rice, special dipping sauces, and garnishes that are served at practically every meal. These basic recipes are part of almost every recipe in the next chapters.

DIPPING SAUCE
Nước Chấm

Get used to this dipping sauce. It is served with *everything!* In almost every Vietnamese home, there is a container of nuoc cham sitting in the refrigerator and a bowl of it on the table. It is amazing how an everyday meal can be transformed into an adventure simply by adding dipping sauce to each bite. Try out this recipe and modify it to your own tastes. You can make variations, for instance, by adding julienned carrots, ginger, or scallions. This recipe usually makes enough sauce for four servings of simple dishes, such as the comfort food dishes in the Asian Garden Mall chapter.

½ fresh Thai bird chile, finely
    chopped into rings, seeds
    included
8 tablespoons warm water
1½ tablespoons sugar
1 clove garlic, finely chopped
3 tablespoons fish sauce
1½ tablespoons fresh lime juice

Whisk together all the ingredients in a small bowl. Make sure the sugar is completely dissolved. Leave the bowl at room temperature for at least several hours before serving. The longer you let the ingredients marinate, the more flavor the sauce will have. If you will not be using the sauce within a day, refrigerate it, because the sugar and lime juice will cause it to spoil. Bring it back to room temperature before serving.

[MAKES 1 CUP]

DIPPING SAUCE WITH GINGER
Nước Chấm Gừng

This is your simple nuoc cham recipe with an extra kick from fresh ginger. It's perfect to brighten up poultry and fish dishes. This recipe usually makes enough sauce for four servings of simple dishes.

4 cloves garlic, minced
1½ tablespoons sugar
1 teaspoon chili paste
¼ cup minced fresh ginger
2 tablespoons fresh lime juice
¼ cup fish sauce
⅔ cup water

In a small bowl, whisk together all the ingredients until the sugar is dissolved. Leave the bowl at room temperature for a few hours to let the sauce marinate. As with dipping sauce, it is best to refrigerate if you are not planning to serve it within 24 hours.

[MAKES 1¼ CUPS]

PEANUT SAUCE
Tương Đậu Phộng

The Vietnamese version of peanut sauce is a little bit sweeter and soupier in texture than other Asian versions such as Thai and Chinese. Because of its sweetness and richness, this peanut sauce is a better complement for spring rolls and other bland foods than nuoc cham. For a bit more kick, add more chili paste.

1 tablespoon peanut oil or
    sesame oil

3 cloves garlic, minced

1/2 cup finely ground unsalted
    dry-roasted peanuts

1/2 teaspoon chili paste

3/4 cup chicken broth

1 1/2 tablespoons thick peanut
    butter

1/3 cup hoisin sauce

1 teaspoon sugar

1 teaspoon fish sauce

1/2 teaspoon cornstarch

2 tablespoons crushed unsalted
    dry-roasted peanuts, for garnish

1. Heat the oil in a small saucepan. Add the minced garlic and cook until it is golden brown. Drain and discard the oil. Set garlic aside.

2. In a small bowl, whisk the cooked garlic with the ground peanuts, chili paste, chicken broth, peanut butter, hoisin sauce, sugar, and fish sauce.

3. When the mixture has a smooth consistency, pour it into the saucepan and bring it to a boil over high heat. Let it boil for 5 minutes, then reduce the heat to a simmer.

4. Add the cornstarch and mix well to a very smooth consistency. Let cool to room temperature. Stir, then garnish with additional crushed peanuts before serving.

[MAKES 2 CUPS]

GINGER LIME SOY SAUCE
Tướng Chanh Gừng

Ginger lime soy sauce is not used often because of its intensity, and soy dipping sauces in general are more Chinese-influenced. Because it's the least subtle of all the dipping sauces, it accompanies poached or boiled meat dishes that are in need of flavor.

¹/₃ cup fresh lime juice

3 tablespoons soy sauce

³/₄ cup water

1 tablespoon roughly chopped
   fresh ginger

¹/₂ teaspoon sugar

1 teaspoon finely chopped garlic

In a small bowl, whisk together all the ingredients until the sugar is dissolved. Leave the bowl at room temperature for a half hour before serving. As with dipping sauce, it is best to refrigerate if you are not planning to serve within the day.

[MAKES 1 CUP]

SCALLION OIL
Dầu Hành

Scallion oil is great to use as a topping for grilled meat and seafood dishes or any kind of rice vermicelli. It can be stored in a covered jar at room temperature for up to a week.

3 scallions, chopped into rings

¹/₂ cup sesame or olive oil

¹/₄ teaspoon salt

In a saucepan or deep skillet, heat the scallions, oil, and salt over medium heat. Cook for 2 minutes. Set aside and allow the oil to cool to room temperature before drizzling it over food.

[MAKES ¹/₂ CUP]

FRIED SHALLOTS AND GARLIC
Hành Chiên and Tỏi Chiên

Many Vietnamese dishes ask for a garnish of fried, thinly sliced shallots or garlic. These are needed not only for presentation but also for their aroma and crunchy texture. As you learn to appreciate this garnish, feel free to use it with any recipes of your choosing.

⅓ cup peanut or sesame oil

2 small shallots or 3 cloves garlic, thinly sliced lengthwise

In a medium skillet, heat the oil until hot. Add the shallots or garlic cloves (or both) and fry until fragrant and golden brown, or about 5 minutes. Remove them with a slotted spoon and drain on paper towels before using them as a garnish.

[MAKES ¼ CUP]

Respect for elders is extremely important in the Vietnamese culture. Not only are elders served first when it comes to food, but you should also expect to give up your seat on a bus or your place in line to an elderly person.

PICKLED CARROTS AND DAIKON
Cải Chua

Pickled carrots and daikon are great to serve, cool or at room temperature, with the salad platter. Diners will gravitate to them if they need a tangy and sweet crunch to complement their meal. Generally served as just an accompaniment, these pickled treats are also added to banh mi thit (sandwiches).

1 cup rice vinegar

1/2 cup water

1 teaspoon salt

2 tablespoons sugar

2 medium carrots, peeled

1/2 pound daikon, peeled

4 whole cloves garlic, peeled

1 Thai bird chile, chopped into rings

1. In a saucepan, bring the vinegar, water, salt, and sugar to a boil. Let boil for 5 minutes. Remove from the heat and set aside to cool.

2. While the vinegar and water mixture is boiling, slice the carrots and daikon into either 1/8-inch slices, or into matchstick pieces—whichever shape you prefer.

3. Put the carrots and daikon in a large jar with the garlic and chile. Add the cooled vinegar mixture. Seal tight and refrigerate for at least 24 hours before eating. The vegetables can be kept up to 3 weeks in the refrigerator.

[MAKES 3 CUPS]

PICKLED SHALLOTS
Củ Kiệu Chua

Packed in vinegar, sugar, and salt, pickled shallots are used as a condiment for grilled foods and to add a sweet-and-sour taste to main dishes. They are often purchased in jars at the grocery store, but it is fun to make your own if you have extra shallots lying around. They should be served cool or at room temperature.

1½ cups rice vinegar

¾ cup water

1 teaspoon salt

2 tablespoons sugar

1 cup whole shallot cloves

2 fresh Thai bird chiles, chopped
   into rings

1. In a saucepan, bring to a boil the rice vinegar, water, salt, and sugar. Let boil for 5 minutes. Remove from heat and set aside to cool.

2. Put the shallot cloves, chiles, and cooled vinegar mixture into a large jar. Seal tight. Let them sit for 48 hours before serving. They will keep up to 4 weeks with refrigeration.

[MAKES 1 CUP]

The 2000 U.S. census found that over the past ten years, the Vietnamese population in the United States grew at a rate of 82.7 percent to 1.2 million, with half residing in California alone. The Vietnamese are the second fastest-growing minority group in the United States; Asian Indians are first.

SALAD PLATTER
Dĩa Xà Lách

One of the most important components of the Vietnamese dining experience is the salad platter. Xa lach, loosely translated, means "salad." The quintessential salad platter (below) is composed of various fresh, leafy herbs, both common ones like mint and cilantro and more Vietnamese herbs such as coriander and perilla. It is the individual herbs that are of particular importance. They each represent a specific flavor—lemony zing, peppery, pungent, sweet—that can be plucked from the platter to match Vietnamese dishes. The basic salad platter also includes red or green leaf lettuce (or any other fresh lettuce), sliced cucumbers, lime wedges to be squeezed over the appropriate dishes, and Thai chiles (left whole on the platter to be broken and shared by the entire group). Sometimes pickled shallots or carrots are included. The salad platter, along with hot steamed rice and dipping sauce, is served at practically every meal. Even with your run-of-the-mill Vietnamese dinner, you need your plate of herbs with your rice. You are forever dipping and wrapping these herbs around foods or adding them straight to your rice or noodle bowl. Make sure everyone's hands are clean! It is really what sets Vietnamese food apart and what makes it so special—that we would demand to have a bite of fresh coriander or Thai basil with each spoonful of plain steamed rice. Each recipe may call for a different composition for the salad platter, and will be so noted.

1/2 cup fresh mint leaves

1/2 cup fresh cilantro leaves

2/3 cup fresh Thai basil leaves

1/3 cup fresh perilla leaves

2/3 cup fresh Vietnamese coriander leaves

1 head red or green leaf lettuce

1 cucumber, peeled and cut into
   1/4-inch slices

6 pickled shallots

2 whole red or green fresh Thai
   bird chiles

1 lime, quartered

1 cup fresh mung bean sprouts

1. Wash all greens and dry.

2. Herbs like mint, cilantro, and basil do not need to be chopped, just separated. Separate the lettuce leaves. Red lettuce needs to be separated but not torn apart.

3. On a large platter arrange all the different components in separate piles. Do not mix anything together. The salad platter is served at the table with the rest of the dishes, family-style. The platter is passed around and diners will take what they need, even breaking off a piece of chile. The lime wedge is especially good with the noodle soups, to be squeezed into the broth for extra taste.

[SERVES 4]

Cơm

Steamed rice is a staple of Vietnamese cuisine. It's best made with a rice cooker, an appliance every Vietnamese person owns, but you can also make it in a nonstick saucepan. It's quite easy. To make light, fluffy, and perfectly cooked rice, use a 1-to-1 ratio for the rice and water. If you are making rice on a stovetop, you will need a bit more water as it will evaporate more quickly than in a rice cooker.

1 1/2 cups uncooked jasmine rice

1 1/2 cups water (add 1/4 cup for stovetop cooking)

1. Rinse the jasmine rice under running water to remove starches, using a fine-mesh strainer or colander. With your hands squeeze rice by the fistfuls to break up the residual starch. Rice needs to be rinsed at least twice until the water runs clear.

2. If you are using a rice cooker, place the rinsed rice in it and add 1 1/2 cups water. Start the rice cooker; serve when all the water is absorbed by the rice.

3. If you are cooking on the stovetop, put the rice and 1 3/4 cups water in a medium-size nonstick saucepan. Bring the pan to a boil and let boil for 5 minutes, uncovered. Stir, then bring the heat down to a simmer. Cover the pot and cook for about 15 minutes, or until the water has been completely absorbed. Stir only once more to break up the rice while cooking.

[SERVES 4]

Meat and poultry dishes are more common in Vietnamese cuisine today than they were in the past, although they are served less frequently than seafood. Because Vietnam is a developing country and largely agrarian, beef, pork, and chicken were not plentiful and came at a high price. So the Vietnamese would salt meat and poultry heavily so that diners would take just small bites along with large quantities of rice to cut the sodium. That way, one meat dish would be able to serve a large number of people.

Bún

The herb noodle salad known as bun is a traditional Vietnamese dish. (Note: *Bun* is also the word for plain rice vermicelli, but in this book we generally use it for herb noodle salad.) On a restaurant menu, there is often a whole section devoted strictly to bun dishes. Bun is often served as its own meal, topped with fresh seafood, grilled meats, and meat pies like cha lua or thit mam. Each geographic region has its own bun recipes. In South Vietnam you will find more seafood-based dishes, for example, while people in Vietnam's central region love their shrimp variations of bun. The recipe here is for a basic bun with some standard garnishes. You will find a number of recipes with grilled meats and seafood that can or should be served with this basic herb noodle salad. Some other easy and flavorful toppings include fresh shrimp (deveined and cut lengthwise), diced tofu, fresh fish, and more vegetables, like braised eggplant, carrots—whatever you like! Bun is best served in individual bowls; if you make one large, family-style bowl, make sure to serve it quickly so that the herbs do not wilt, or wait until the last minute to add the dipping sauce.

½ pound (approximately 2 small packages) rice vermicelli

¾ cup fresh mung bean sprouts

½ cup julienned cucumber

½ cup shredded fresh Vietnamese coriander leaves

½ cup roughly chopped fresh mint or peppermint leaves

⅓ cup roughly chopped fresh cilantro leaves

½ cup roughly chopped fresh Thai basil leaves

2 scallions, chopped into rings

¼ cup fried sliced garlic

1 teaspoon ground black pepper

½ cup crushed unsalted dry-roasted peanuts

⅓ cup dipping sauce (nuoc cham)

1. Fill a large pot with water and bring it to a rolling boil. Turn off the pot and add the vermicelli noodles. Thin rice noodles cook very quickly, so let them sit in the hot water for only 2 minutes. Drain, rinse with cold water, and set aside to cool in a colander. Or you can fill a bowl with hot tap water and let the noodles sit for 15 minutes before draining. When cooked, the noodles should be soft and will slightly stick together.

2. Divide the noodles into four bowls. Divide the bean sprouts, cucumber, coriander leaves, mint, cilantro, and Thai basil into fourths, and put them on top of each serving of noodles. You can either pile them on top of each other or separate them into individual parts.

3. Garnish the bowls with the scallions, fried garlic, black pepper, and peanuts, and any other toppings you wish.

4. Before serving, pour the dipping sauce over each serving and toss before eating.

[SERVES 4]

BOILED PEANUTS
Đậu Phộng

Lightly salted boiled peanuts are considered a wonderful, addictive snack by the Vietnamese. They should be eaten right away because they do not keep for very long.

2 cups raw peanuts, with shells

4 cups water

2 tablespoons salt

1. Wash the peanuts thoroughly in a colander under running warm water. Then soak them in a bowl of cool water for about 15 minutes.

2. Drain the peanuts and put them in a large saucepan. Cover them with the 4 cups of water, and add 1 tablespoon of the salt. On medium heat, let the peanuts cook at a rolling boil for a total of 30 minutes, uncovered. Add another tablespoon of salt after the first 15 minutes of boiling. (The salt is not added all at once because the shells tend to absorb it too quickly.)

3. Drain and serve warm with a bowl to put the shells in.

[MAKES 2 CUPS]

RECIPES

A DRIVE DOWN BOLSA AVENUE

Salads and Soups

THE VIETNAMESE MARKETS

At eight o'clock every morning, seven days a week, crowds of people begin to gather in the grocery stores of Little Saigon, which are scattered along Bolsa Avenue and Westminster Boulevard. More than 2,500 customers will shop at any given market on a weekday; the number increases to 3,500 on a Saturday or Sunday. By evening most markets will have sold all their fresh produce and meats and fish.

Though predominantly Asian, the markets' customer base represents a mix of people from nearby neighborhoods and cities, with shoppers coming from as far away as Los Angeles and San Diego Counties. For the residents of Little Saigon, the markets are an important source of Vietnamese and other Asian products as well as the place to go for low prices. For the tourist, the markets' ethnic appeal and diversity of exotic products make them fascinating to explore.

Entering the markets of Little Saigon is like stepping into another country, or at the very least a cultural crossroads. Along the periphery of the stores, local Vietnamese bakeries and tofu and soy makers sell their branded, freshly made goods, and older women sell their homemade simple snacks, such as sticky Vietnamese treats wrapped in banana leaves. You'll find a whole aisle displaying more than fifty varieties of fish sauce and an adjacent aisle with almost every kind of dried Asian noodle you can imagine. But then you'll discover Arm & Hammer baking soda boxes stacked among Chinese products like tapioca starch and MSG—a reminder that you are still in America. In the freezer section, vegetarian and soy-based meat substitutes are sold along with Häagen-Dazs ice cream and frozen pizzas. The market is also a good place to find inexpensive and useful tools and equipment for the Vietnamese kitchen including chopsticks, three-tier steamers, plastic mandolines, clay pots, cleavers, and rice bowls.

The markets' main appeal is the wide array of exotic vegetables, fruits, and herbs that would be unavailable or rarely found in other grocery stores. Almost a third of the space in every market is dedicated to the vegetables, fruits, and herbs section. Some people claim that the quality and quantity of fresh produce in these markets cannot be duplicated anywhere else.

In this chapter you will find recipes that highlight the very best of both the exotic and the more ordinary produce found in these Vietnamese markets. The dishes showcase the Vietnamese reliance on and appreciation for the freshest of herbs and vegetables. Recipes for fresh salads and vegetable consommés (canh) utilize the ingredients found in the produce section of any Little Saigon market. Any of these recipes can be made vegetarian by taking out the meat or fish or, if desired, by substituting tofu.

The Asian supermarket business is extremely competitive, much like the restaurant business in Little Saigon. But the success of the existing markets makes entrepreneurs salivate, so new grocery stores do appear once in a while, with a whole lot of fanfare. Not only do grocers stay competitive by offering the best prices, but they also lure customers with gifts based on the amount spent in the store. Sometimes it's a bag of rice or some fish sauce—or even a rice cooker for the big spenders.

TRADITIONAL SHREDDED CHICKEN AND CABBAGE SALAD
Gỏi Gà

Goi ga, regarded as the coleslaw of South Vietnam, is a refreshingly sweet and tangy salad. The chopping and slicing steps to make it may seem laborious, but they're necessary to let all the ingredients be more evenly coated by the dressing. Note that each part of the salad is dressed separately before the final tossing. There are a number of ways this salad can be expanded, such as by adding boiled shrimp and pork, more cucumber slices, shallots, or other cabbages (except red cabbage). Just make sure you have the dressing perfected—a balance of tangy, sweet, and salty flavors—as it is the clincher to creating the invigorating taste of goi ga. The fish sauce should not be overwhelming. Serve this salad at room temperature.

3 tablespoons fresh lime juice

4 cloves garlic, finely chopped

1 dried Thai bird chile, thinly sliced

1 tablespoon sugar

5 tablespoons fish sauce

1/2 cup paper-thin slices yellow onion

1 head green cabbage (savoy or napa recommended)

2 medium carrots, peeled

2 chicken breasts (approximately 1 pound total)

1 medium cucumber, peeled and julienned

3 tablespoons finely chopped fresh cilantro leaves

1/2 cup finely chopped fresh Vietnamese coriander leaves

1/4 cup finely chopped fresh mint leaves

1/2 cup crushed lightly salted peanuts

1. In a small bowl, combine the lime juice, chopped garlic, sliced chile, sugar, and fish sauce. Whisk until the sugar is dissolved. Add the sliced onions and set aside.

2. Shred the cabbage and carrots with a mandoline into a large bowl. Pour half of the dressing over the vegetables and let them marinate for at least 15 minutes.

3. Boil the chicken breasts in salted water until fully cooked. Let cool, then shred into thin pieces by hand.

4. Add the chicken, cucumber, cilantro, coriander, and mint to the marinated cabbage and carrots. Add the rest of the dressing and toss. Let the salad sit for about 10 minutes before serving to allow the cabbage to wilt a bit.

5. In a skillet over high heat, toast the crushed peanuts. Add them to the top of the salad as a garnish just before serving.

[SERVES 6]

Gỏi Đu Đủ

Not only is this a fragrant salad with herbs and spices, but it is also a great combination of tangy and sweet flavors with the umami taste of shellfish and fish sauce. It takes some effort to julienne a huge papaya, but the dish is worth it. If you can't find green papaya anywhere, even in a huge Asian supermarket, hard, unripened green mangoes make a good substitute. Traditionally, the dish is served with kho bo, dried seasoned beef similar to jerky but more tender. Besides beef, this salad can be served with a number of other accompaniments such as grilled shrimp or even tofu.

Juice of 1 small lime

2 cloves garlic, minced

1 teaspoon sugar

2 tablespoons fish sauce

$\frac{1}{2}$ fresh Thai bird chile, finely
   chopped

1 tablespoon oil

1 tablespoon minced shallots

1 green papaya or 2 green
   mangoes

$\frac{1}{2}$ cup chopped fresh Vietnamese
   coriander leaves

$\frac{1}{3}$ cup plus $\frac{1}{4}$ cup chopped fresh
   Thai basil leaves

$\frac{1}{3}$ pound cooked shrimp, cleaned,
   deveined, sliced lengthwise

3 tablespoons finely chopped
   unsalted dry-roasted peanuts

1. In a small bowl, combine the lime juice, garlic, sugar, fish sauce, and chopped chile. Whisk until the sugar is dissolved.

2. In a small skillet or saucepan, heat the oil. Fry the minced shallots until golden brown. Drain and add to the fish sauce mixture.

3. Julienne the papaya or mangoes into thin, matchstick strips 2 inches long, and place them in a large serving bowl or platter. Pour the dressing all over the strips, evenly coating them. Toss with $\frac{1}{4}$ cup of the chopped coriander and $\frac{1}{3}$ cup of the Thai basil.

4. Top the dressed papaya with the cooked shrimp, and garnish with the peanuts, the remaining $\frac{1}{4}$ cup coriander, and the remaining $\frac{1}{4}$ cup basil. You can prepare this salad up to an hour before serving, but no longer or the herbs will wilt.

[SERVES 4]

As with most Asian salads, our dressings do not include a generous use of oil. In fact, almost all Vietnamese dressings involve simply a combination of vinegar, sugar, lime, and chile. The julienned and thin-shredded vegetables bring out the natural juices and flavors of many of the salads.

Gỏi Bò

Don't be intimidated by the long list of ingredients here. This dish will make any carnivore eager to eat his veggies again. The meat, tender and sweet, is arranged neatly over this salad made lively by Thai basil, mint, sprouts, shallots, onions, cucumbers, and lemongrass. Unlike the chicken goi with cabbage, you do not want to pour the vinaigrette over the salad until just before serving.

$1/4$ cup fish sauce

1 tablespoon sugar

$1/4$ cup fresh lime juice

$1 1/2$ teaspoons ground black pepper

1 teaspoon salt

1 teaspoon chili paste

2 tablespoons finely chopped fresh lemongrass

3 tablespoons olive oil

1 medium onion, sliced in half rings

7 cloves garlic, finely chopped

1 pound top sirloin steak or filet

$1/2$ cup roughly chopped fresh Thai basil leaves

3 cups shredded iceberg lettuce

1 small cucumber, peeled and julienned

$1/2$ cup roughly chopped fresh mint leaves

1 cup fresh mung bean sprouts

$1/4$ cup fried shallots

$1/3$ cup crushed unsalted dry-roasted peanuts

1. In a small bowl, whisk together the fish sauce, sugar, lime juice, black pepper, salt, chili paste, and lemongrass until the sugar is completely dissolved. Set aside.

2. Heat the oil in a skillet over high heat. When it is hot, add the onions and garlic and cook for about 5 minutes.

3. Meanwhile, slice the steak into thin, $1/2$-inch slices against the grain. Add the slices to the hot skillet and immediately pour in the fish sauce vinaigrette. Sauté the steak, tossing it in the vinaigrette, for just another 2 minutes for rare doneness (or longer as desired).

4. Put the steak and vinaigrette into a medium bowl and set aside.

5. In a large salad bowl, combine the Thai basil, lettuce, cucumber, mint leaves, and bean sprouts. Take about 5 tablespoons of the vinaigrette from the meat, and drizzle it over the salad. Toss well.

6. Put the salad on a large platter and top it with the slices of steak. Drizzle any remaining steak juices and vinaigrette on top. Garnish with the fried shallots and roasted peanuts.

[SERVES 4]

Bôbô's Dầu Giấm

Bô is the word for "father," and growing up we called my dad Bobo. Here is Bobo's simple dressing for a salad. Think of the salad platter thrown into a bowl. Bobo's dressing is delicious, balanced, and a perfect vinaigrette.

$1/2$ cup rice vinegar

$1/2$ cup olive oil

$1/2$ onion, thinly sliced

1 clove garlic, chopped

$1/2$ tablespoon sugar

1 teaspoon ground black pepper

1 tablespoon Maggi Seasoning
  Sauce

In a small bowl, whisk together the rice vinegar and olive oil. Add the remaining ingredients, whisk together, and let sit for at least 10 minutes. Toss the dressing over any fresh salad.

[MAKES 1$1/4$ CUPS]

There are a few things in Little Saigon that reveal the humble origins of the inhabitants, and the Vietnamese market is certainly one of them. In the early days of Little Saigon, the residents depended on the grocers to feed them cheaply. Food stamps coupled with substantially cheaper goods than those found at large grocery chains provided not only nourishment for many locals, but also a chance to save money and eventually step away from welfare programs. Times are much better in Little Saigon now, though, and many people's fortunes have turned around.

Canh Bắp Cải Thịt Tom

You probably never gave cabbage much thought, but now, cooking Vietnamese food, you'll need to. Between cabbage salads and cabbage soups, you can quickly see how versatile an otherwise bland vegetable can be. In this recipe cabbage takes on a satiny texture after being cooked in a flavorful stock with pork and shrimp. This soup is intended to be just a canh—a consommé side dish served as a liquid refreshment—but I can easily consume this soup as a whole meal by itself.

6 cups homemade or purchased
   chicken stock

⅓ pound fresh shrimp, peeled
   and deveined

6 cloves garlic

⅓ cup fish sauce

½ tablespoon salt

1 tablespoon ground black pepper

1 large green cabbage, cleaned,
   leaves separated

⅓ pound lean ground pork

4 scallions, sliced into rings

1. In a large stockpot, bring the chicken stock to a boil.

2. In a food processor, mince the shrimp, garlic, and 1 tablespoon of the fish sauce together. Scrape the mixture into a large bowl and add the salt and black pepper. Combine thoroughly and set aside.

3. Cut the cabbage into 2-inch strips. Add the cabbage strips and the remaining fish sauce to the boiling chicken stock and cook for 5 minutes. Lower the heat to a simmer.

4. Add the ground pork to the soup, using a fork or whisk to break it up so that it is evenly distributed. You do not want meatballs in the soup.

5. Then add the ground shrimp mixture, dropping it into the soup in large teaspoon-size lumps. Continue simmering on low for another 5 minutes or until the shrimp and pork are completely cooked.

6. Stir in the sliced scallions and serve immediately.

[SERVES 6]

Canh, literally translated as "soup," is a consommé or broth that is a necessary part of any Vietnamese meal. During the meal it's the canh that's imbibed to help wash down the rice and salty main dishes. Generally you can add whatever you like to a canh. Normally it begins with a basic stock—usually a chicken or pork broth—or even just fish sauce and water. A vegetable is added to complete the soup, along with reconstituted shrimp or small pieces of meat taken from the bones used to prepare the stock.

Canh Cải Tàu Tom

Here's another favorite canh. It includes mustard greens, which are great in a canh because they have a mild taste when cooked and they keep their texture. Tamarind pulp is another good ingredient to use in canh, as it provides a light sweet-and-tart taste. Rice paddy flower is popular with shrimp and fish soups because its strong, perfumed fragrance covers up the fishiness that some may not find palatable. If you have the time, add some dried shrimp to the recipe. When you put just a few tablespoons of the liquid from the reconstituted shrimp into the soup, the soup will turn into something briny and magical.

6 cups water

2 tablespoons tamarind pulp

1/2 pound fresh shrimp, peeled and deveined

4 cloves garlic

1 tablespoon sugar

1 tablespoon ground black pepper

1/4 cup fish sauce

1 bunch fresh mustard greens, or 4 cups, leaves only

1/2 cup rice paddy flower

1 cup fresh mung bean sprouts

1. In a large stockpot, bring the water and the tamarind pulp to a boil. Once the water begins to boil, stir well to dissolve and distribute the pulp through the broth. Allow the broth to boil for 10 minutes before bringing it down to a simmer.

2. Meanwhile, in a food processor or with a mortar and pestle, mix together the shrimp, garlic, sugar, and black pepper.

3. Add the ground shrimp mixture by the tablespoonful to the simmering broth. Let it cook for about 3 minutes, or until the shrimp is cooked. Stir in the fish sauce.

4. Add the mustard greens and rice paddy flower. Cook for another 10 minutes, then add the bean sprouts and serve.

[SERVES 4]

My grandma has taught me that to get the right prices at Little Saigon markets, you need to keep your fingers on the pulse of what's being delivered every day. She does this through her network of elderly women friends in the community. Someone must know someone who is a cousin of someone who runs the food delivery trucks.

Canh Bàu Tom

Winter melon is rather bland when cooked alone, but there is nothing quite like its deep, sweet, refreshing flavor in a canh or a stir-fry. It is easily chopped and quickly cooked. There are little whiskers on the skin of the melon, so my family prefers to lightly peel it before cooking.

8 cups water

3 tablespoons dried shrimp

$1/4$ cup fish sauce

3 cloves garlic

$1/3$ pound fresh shrimp, shells removed and deveined

$1/2$ tablespoon salt

$1^1/2$ tablespoons ground black pepper

$1/2$ tablespoon sugar

1 tablespoon olive oil

1 large green winter melon (bau), lightly peeled, cut in half length-wise, and sliced into $1/2$-inch slices

1 scallion, chopped into rings

1. In a medium stockpot, boil the water with the dried shrimp, fish sauce, and garlic for 15 minutes.

2. While the water is boiling, pound the fresh shrimp with a mortar and pestle or process in a food processor. Put in a small bowl. Add the salt, pepper, sugar, and olive oil to the bowl. Blend well.

3. Drop the shrimp paste into the boiling water a few tablespoonfuls at a time. It will cook immediately and appear like pink dumplings in the water.

4. Add the sliced winter melon to the stockpot and boil for another 15 minutes. Serve when the winter melon is very tender.

5. Ladle all of the soup into a large bowl, add the scallions, and serve family-style with other dishes.

[SERVES 4]

Xúp Măng Cua

Asparagus was introduced to the Vietnamese cuisine by the French, so it is not found in many traditional Vietnamese recipes. But today this soup is a popular item on the banquet menu. If fresh asparagus and crabmeat are not available, you can use canned, but fresh ingredients are always preferred by the Vietnamese. Look for lump crabmeat from the body of the crab. The most difficult part of this otherwise simple dish is making sure the egg whites are properly whipped into the soup. The presentation should be that of gentle clouds floating in the soup.

6 cups chicken stock (homemade or purchased)

3 tablespoons fish sauce

1 tablespoon sugar

3 cloves garlic, minced

3 shallots, finely chopped

2 tablespoons sesame seed oil

3/4 cup lump crabmeat

1 teaspoon salt

1 teaspoon ground black pepper

2 tablespoons oyster sauce

8 stalks fresh asparagus, white or green, cut into 1 1/2-inch pieces

1/3 cup finely chopped tree ear mushrooms

2 1/2 tablespoons cornstarch

4 egg whites

Chopped fresh cilantro leaves

2 scallions, chopped into rings

1. Bring the chicken stock to a rolling boil in a large stockpot. Add the fish sauce and sugar and stir well. Boil for another 15 minutes. Lower heat and simmer.

2. In a medium skillet, sauté the garlic and shallots in the sesame seed oil for a few minutes. Add the crabmeat, salt, pepper, and oyster sauce and sauté for about 5 minutes. Then add the mixture directly to the stockpot and stir well to break up the crabmeat.

3. Add the chopped asparagus and mushrooms to the stockpot and stir well. After a few minutes, slowly stir in the cornstarch to thicken the soup. Simmer for another 15 minutes.

4. Just before serving, swirl the soup in a circular motion and add the egg whites slowly so that they cook in threadlike pieces—you do not want chunks of scrambled egg in the soup. If you stir the egg whites in too quickly, they'll blend in too much and become lost in the soup.

5. Ladle the soup into bowls and garnish each serving with the cilantro, scallions, and a dash of black pepper.

[SERVES 6]

Simple Comfort Foods

THE ASIAN GARDEN MALL AND MOM-AND-POP RESTAURANTS

Most Americans think of comfort food as macaroni and cheese, clam chowder, or meat loaf—foods evocative of good and happy times, cozy childhoods, and cheerful family meals around the kitchen table. Vietnamese cuisine has its own set of comfort dishes—rice porridge, curry, spiced beef stew, and others—all easy-to-make foods whose mere mention makes everyone happier. My grandmother remembers a time when comfort food came only from the home kitchen. But today these dishes are on the menus of many of the restaurants in Little Saigon.

Locals know exactly where to go for specific dishes and what to order without even glancing at the menu. Visitors who are not familiar with the food can ask for a menu with pictures. If they are still uncertain as to what to order, they can trust their waiter or waitress to name the best dishes at the restaurant, the chef's specialty, or what the cook attends to first thing in the morning. Some of these mom-and-pop restaurants are so busy and popular that once in a while you will be asked to sit with complete strangers. Though these restaurants may be considered "holes-in-the-wall," many restaurateurs realize that Vietnamese Americans are comfortable with the simple atmosphere. In fact, most restaurants look exactly the same as when they opened several decades ago.

The Asian Garden Mall, named Phuc Loc Tho (Luck, Fortune, and Longevity), is another place to find comfort foods in Little Saigon. This 150,000-square-foot indoor mall on Bolsa Avenue has a bustling oval-shaped food court on the ground floor. Freshly prepared snacks and simple dishes rest under bright heat lamps behind a glass enclosure. The foods mirror those sold in the market stalls of Saigon's famous Ben Thanh Market, where scores of vendors bring their homemade dishes to sell. The Asian Garden Mall is especially busy on the weekends, as both locals and tourists hurry about the food court with their red trays, pointing or shouting for the desired food. They then eat at tables behind a brass rail separating the dining area from the rest of the pedestrian traffic at the mall. Once the meal is completed, it's back to shopping in the mall's 300 retail spaces for clothing, jewelry, Oriental gifts, and video and music items.

The recipes in this chapter reflect the simple dishes found in the casual restaurants in Little Saigon as well as in the Asian Garden Mall's food court. Other comfort foods are the caramelized and braised dishes, or kho, found in the Festive Holiday Foods chapter.

Banh mi (bread) delis are found all over Little Saigon; there are three in the Asian Garden Mall alone. Banh mi thit are Vietnamese sandwiches, which are rapidly growing in popularity—it's the next big Vietnamese food item after pho. It is hard for anyone to resist biting into a light and crispy crust (better than any French baguette) and tasting the warm bread, cool cold cuts, and crunchy vegetables. Banh mi dac biet, "the special," is on the menu at every deli. It incorporates all the Vietnamese cold cuts. The meat may seem a bit odd, but rest assured that it's all pork—a blend of lean and fatty parts. Other varieties of sandwiches include barbecued pork, chicken, and vegetarian. Julienned carrots and daikon marinated in vinegar, fresh cilantro, cucumber slices, and slices of fresh jalapeños provide a nice, tangy crunch to each sandwich.

CHICKEN WITH GINGER AND GARLIC RICE
Cơm Gà

This comfort food dish is generally made when certain leftovers are around the kitchen—cooked chicken, chicken stock, and cooked rice—but it's also widely available in delis and many of Little Saigon's more casual restaurants. This recipe may seem overly simplistic for the more adventurous, but the rice is fragrant and robust from the garlic and ginger, and the dipping sauce is a real highlight. Tofu or vegetables can be substituted for the chicken if desired.

6 tablespoons olive oil

5 cloves garlic, minced

½ fresh Thai bird chile, finely chopped

3 tablespoons peeled, finely chopped fresh ginger

4 cups cooked, dry, long-grain rice

⅓ cup chicken stock

¼ cup fish sauce

⅓ pound cooked chicken meat (about half the meat of a medium chicken), warmed

¼ cup roughly chopped fresh mint leaves

Dipping Sauce with Ginger (see recipe in Basics)

1. In a large skillet or pot, warm the oil over high heat. When it is hot, add the garlic, chile, and ginger, and cook for 3 minutes or until fragrant.

2. Add the cooked rice and stir constantly for about 5 minutes. Some of the rice may begin to char or become crispy, but this step is necessary to dry out the rice a little.

3. Add the chicken stock to the rice and stir. Then add the fish sauce and continue stirring. Reduce the heat and cook for another 15 minutes, uncovered, or until the liquid has reduced. Stir occasionally so that the rice does not burn.

4. While the rice is cooking, cut the warm chicken in slices. Spoon the rice into individual bowls and top each serving with a few slices of chicken, mint leaves, and a few spoonfuls of the ginger dipping sauce.

[SERVES 4]

CHICKEN CURRY WITH POTATOES AND PEAS
Cà-rí Gà

Every Southeast Asian cuisine has its own version of curry, but the Vietnamese chicken curry is my favorite because it is less stewlike than other curries and has a wonderful flavor of coconut milk and subtle spices. My grandma's recipe here is the best example of Vietnamese curry I know. The South Vietnamese like using yams, and the curry powder meshes well with the yams' sugary goodness.

2 stalks fresh or dried lemongrass, cut into 2-inch lengths

2 tablespoons yellow curry powder

3 cloves garlic

1 tablespoon sugar

2 shallots

2 tablespoons salt

1 tablespoon chili paste (less if you want a milder flavor)

5 tablespoons vegetable or canola oil

1 tablespoon ground black pepper

1 1/2 pounds skinless chicken thighs and drumsticks

1 1/2 yellow onions, chopped into 6 pieces and separated

1 bay leaf

2 1/2 cups water

2 cups coconut milk

3 large carrots, cut into 1-inch pieces

3 pounds yams, peeled and sliced into 1 1/2-inch pieces
   (white potatoes can be substituted)

1 1/2 cups frozen or canned peas

1/4 cup chopped fresh cilantro leaves

Orchids prosper in the Vietnamese climate, growing both wild and in homes all over the country. Many of the world's rarest and most valuable orchids can be found in Vietnam. In Little Saigon the blooms are sold in practically every color all year-round. You can find them on stands at the Asian Garden Mall, on the sidewalks, in the grocery stores, and even at a restaurant or bakery. Orchids are especially abundant during Tet, along with many other flowers and cherry blossom branches.

1. If using dried lemongrass, remove its rough outer leaves with your hands until you see fresh green layers. Soak in warm water for up to 30 minutes to soften the herb.

2. In a food processor, combine curry powder, garlic, sugar, shallots, salt, chili paste, 1 tablespoon of the oil, and black pepper. Lightly pulse and process into a rough paste. (The traditional version of this curry calls for using a mortar and pestle, but the food processor works fine here.)

3. Rub the paste all over the chicken with your hands. Put the chicken in a bowl, cover, and refrigerate for at least an hour.

4. In a large stockpot, heat the remaining oil over medium heat and cook the onion for 5 minutes. Add the bay leaf and lemongrass and cook for another few minutes.

5. Remove the chicken from the refrigerator. Add it to the stockpot and sear it with the lemongrass, onion, and bay leaf. Let the chicken cook for 10 to 15 minutes or until it is browned.

6. Add the water, coconut milk, carrots, and potatoes to the pot. Bring to a rolling boil and cook for 5 minutes. Bring down to a simmer and cook for another 15 minutes. (If you want to shorten the cooking time, parboil the carrots and potatoes before adding them to the pot.) Test the carrots and potatoes to make sure they are cooked through before adding the peas. Continue to cook for another 5 minutes at a light simmer.

7. Serve hot over rice or with fresh, warm baguettes. Garnish with the chopped cilantro. If any curry is left over, refrigerate it immediately, as coconut milk tends to spoil very quickly. The curry will be even more flavorful the next day. Reheat just the amount of curry you will be eating, either in the microwave or on the stove.

[SERVES 8]

Cháo Gà

Chao, also known as congee, is the Vietnamese version of porridge. The soupy rice mixture can be made plain and served with a variety of accompaniments such as salted duck eggs or Chinese sausage. It can also be made with beef, chicken, pork, fish, or shrimp cooked into the porridge, and garlic, ginger, scallions, and cilantro used as flavorings or garnishes. Chao will cure whatever ails you. The blend of hot chicken broth with the medicinal qualities of lemongrass is a cure for your aches and pains. Generally, chao is not served with much meat, but you can add more shredded chicken to your liking.

4 cups unsalted chicken broth
   (purchased or homemade)

5 tablespoons fish sauce

2 tablespoons finely chopped
   fresh ginger

2 stalks fresh lemongrass,
   chopped in 2-inch lengths

1/2 tablespoon sugar

1 tablespoon salt

1 tablespoon black peppercorns

2 cups uncooked jasmine rice

1/2 pound chicken, poached

2 scallions, chopped into rings

1/3 cup chopped fresh cilantro
   leaves

1/4 cup chopped fresh Vietnamese
   coriander leaves

1 cup fresh mung bean sprouts

1/2 yellow onion, finely sliced into
   rings with mandoline

1 lime, quartered

1. Pour the chicken broth into a large stockpot. Bring it to a rolling boil, and add the fish sauce, ginger, lemongrass, sugar, salt, and peppercorns. Stir the broth, and let it simmer for 15 minutes on medium heat.

2. Add the rice and cook for about 35 minutes, covered, or until the rice is almost translucent. The consistency should be similar to that of porridge and a little watery.

3. Remove and discard the bones and skin from the poached chicken. Shred the chicken with your hands. Remove the lemongrass and, if desired, the pieces of ginger.

4. Serve the porridge, very hot, in individual bowls. Place a few pieces of the shredded chicken over the porridge, followed by some chopped scallions, chopped cilantro, chopped Vietnamese coriander, bean sprouts, and some thinly sliced onion rings. Squeeze some lime juice over each portion. Or you can put these garnish items on a separate plate, and allow your guests to garnish their own bowls of porridge.

[SERVES 4]

Cháo Bò

The beef version of chao is made flavorful and fragrant with cilantro, ginger, and lemongrass with a dash of pepper.

6 cups unsalted chicken broth
(purchased or homemade)

5 tablespoons fish sauce

2 thick slices fresh ginger

2 stalks fresh lemongrass, cut into
4-inch lengths

$\frac{1}{2}$ tablespoon sugar

1 tablespoon salt

1 tablespoon ground black pepper

4 cups uncooked jasmine rice

$\frac{1}{2}$ pound lean ground beef

2 scallions, chopped into rings

$\frac{1}{3}$ cup chopped fresh cilantro
leaves

1 cup fresh mung bean sprouts

$\frac{1}{2}$ yellow onion, finely sliced into
rings with mandoline

2 red Thai bird chiles, finely
chopped

1. Warm the chicken broth in a large stockpot over medium heat. Add the fish sauce, ginger, lemongrass, sugar, salt, and pepper. Stir until the sugar and salt are dissolved. Add the uncooked rice and cover. Cook over low heat for about 35 minutes or until the rice is completely done. The consistency should be similar to that of porridge and a little watery.

2. Remove the lemongrass and ginger and continue simmering. Add the ground beef to the pot and stir well to mix the bits of meat through the porridge. Cook over low heat for another 1 to $1\frac{1}{2}$ hours, or until the rice is almost translucent. The porridge should be very watery.

3. Serve very hot in individual bowls, topped with some chopped scallions, chopped cilantro, bean sprouts, and thinly sliced onion rings. Or you can arrange these garnish items on a separate plate, with the chopped Thai bird chiles, and allow your guests to garnish their own rice porridge.

[SERVES 8]

There are some popular delis in Little Saigon where you can order simple chao to go. The most common form of chao found in sit-down restaurants is chao huyet—rice porridge with liver, congealed pork blood, and long intestine (pork "sausage"), accompanied by a deep-fried breadstick.

Thịt Bò Kho

One of my favorite "slow" dishes, this beef stew is more like a perfectly spiced soup than an actual thick stew. Nonetheless, it is still a hearty meal with remarkable flavor and perfect for eating with a fresh, warm baguette to sop up the liquid (steamed white rice is also good). A friend of mine describes it as eating an "exoticized beef stew." The preparation is quite simple, and then you can just leave the stew at the back of your stove in a low simmer for a few hours. Surprisingly, this dish is quite popular for breakfast.

5 tablespoons olive or vegetable oil

1½ teaspoons annatto seeds

1 pound top round beef chuck, cut into 1½-inch cubes

1 fresh Thai bird chile, finely chopped

1½ tablespoons sugar

1 tablespoon yellow curry powder

½ teaspoon salt

¼ cup fish sauce

1 teaspoon ground black pepper

1 large onion, cut into 6 pieces and separated

6 cloves garlic, minced

2 stalks fresh lemongrass, cut into 2-inch lengths

3 star anise pods

6 cups unsalted chicken or beef broth

1 cinnamon stick

2 large carrots, peeled, cut lengthwise, and chopped into 1½-inch pieces

1 medium daikon, peeled and cut into 1½-inch pieces

Fresh cilantro or parsley

1. In a skillet or small saucepan, heat 3 tablespoons of the olive or vegetable oil with the annatto seeds. Stir constantly until the seeds have completely bled their reddish color into the oil. Let cool, then discard the seeds, and set the annatto oil aside.

2. In a large bowl, combine the cubed beef, chopped chile, sugar, curry powder, salt, fish sauce, pepper, and remaining olive or vegetable oil. Cover and refrigerate for at least 30 minutes.

3. Heat the annatto oil in a large stockpot. When it is hot, add the onion, garlic, lemongrass, and anise pods and sauté for 5 minutes.

4. Remove the beef from the bowl, and add it and its marinade to the stockpot. Pour in the chicken or beef broth. Add the cinnamon stick, carrots, and daikon and boil for 5 minutes, then reduce to a very low heat and cook for about 1½ to 2 hours. The meat is done when it's extremely tender or falling apart at the touch. Before serving, remove the lemongrass, anise pods, and cinnamon stick.

5. Serve the stew in individual bowls with warm baguettes, or ladle it over steamed rice. Garnish with fresh cilantro or parsley.

[SERVES 4]

GRILLED BEEF WITH LEMONGRASS AND GARLIC
Bún Bò Nướng Xã Tỏi

The zing of the lemongrass and the heat of the garlic make this grilled beef recipe a very flavorful, fragrant dish. Easy to make in under an hour, the beef is delicious with an herb noodle salad, steamed rice, or rice vermicelli; over a bed of Bibb lettuce and tomatoes; or alone with nuoc cham. You can also skewer the beef cubes as kebabs or even pan-fry them in a skillet to be served as appetizers.

1 teaspoon sugar

1 tablespoon ground black pepper

4 cloves garlic, minced

2 stalks fresh lemongrass, very finely chopped

¼ cup fish sauce

3 tablespoons olive oil

1 pound beef sirloin tip or beef round, sliced thinly

1 yellow onion, quartered

Fresh cilantro or scallions

¼ cup crushed unsalted dry-roasted peanuts

1. First prepare the marinade. In a shallow bowl, stir together the sugar, black pepper, garlic, lemongrass, fish sauce, and 2 tablespoons of the olive oil. Stir until the salt and sugar have dissolved.

2. Place the beef slices in a shallow dish or bowl or a ziplock bag. Pour on the marinade and toss the beef so that it is completely covered. Cover the dish or seal the bag and refrigerate for a half hour.

3. Coat the surface of a grill pan or skillet with the remaining oil. Or prepare a gas or charcoal grill. Start by sautéing or grilling the yellow onion quarters. When they are golden brown, add the beef to the onions. For a skillet or grill pan, pour any remaining marinade over the beef; if using a grill, continue basting the meat with the remaining marinade. The meat will cook within 5 minutes for a medium-rare doneness. Cook according to your preference.

4. To serve, place the hot sliced beef and onions over your accompaniment of choice (herb noodle salad, rice, or plain rice vermicelli) in four separate bowls. Top with the juices from the skillet or grill pan. Serve with generous amounts of nuoc cham, and garnish with cilantro or scallions and crushed peanuts.

[SERVES 4 WITH BUN AS AN ENTREE, 6 AS AN APPETIZER]

Bún Bò Thịt

The idea of honey and beef might concern you at first, but your worries will wash away before you even take your first bite. The aroma of the seared meat with the fragrant cooked honey is only the beginning. Both the honey and the hoisin sauce give the beef a deliciously dark, caramelized flavor, while the lemongrass, chile, and dipping sauce balance the sweetness. The thick sauce adheres well to slippery ingredients such as bun, which this dish should be served over. Grilled beef can also be presented as an appetizer over greens, for a nontraditional Vietnamese meal.

3 tablespoons fish sauce

1 tablespoon hoisin sauce

1 fresh Thai bird chile, finely
  chopped

2 tablespoons honey or sugar

1 teaspoon black pepper

3 stalks fresh lemongrass, very
  finely chopped

1 1/2 tablespoons oil

3 cloves garlic, finely chopped

3/4 pound top sirloin or beef tenderloin, sliced in 1/2-inch slices
  across the grain

1. In a small bowl, whisk together the fish sauce, hoisin sauce, chopped chile, honey or sugar, pepper, and lemongrass until the honey or sugar is dissolved.

2. Heat the olive oil in a skillet or grill over medium heat. Begin by sautéing the chopped garlic for a few minutes.

3. When the garlic is golden brown, add the sliced beef to the skillet and pour the marinade over it, stirring quickly. Cook the meat in its juices and the marinade for about 8 minutes for a medium-well doneness. Adjust the cooking time based on your own preference.

4. Serve the grilled meat hot with an herb noodle salad (bun) or steamed rice, the salad platter, and plenty of nuoc cham.

[SERVES 4 AS AN ENTREE, 6 AS AN APPETIZER]

New restaurants in Little Saigon employ the gimmick of offering free beverages or a $1.00 bowl of pho. My parents' generation has become obsessed with this and will ask at any restaurant in Little Saigon, "What are you giving us for free today?"

Bún Thịt Heo Nướng

This dish is typical of the way the Vietnamese marinate and cook their meats. Served with the fresh herbs, and presented with the contrasting textures of the juicy meat and the soft, thin rice noodles, this is an entree that easily becomes a favorite of first-time diners of Vietnamese cuisine. Steamed rice can be substituted for the herb noodle salad if you prefer. Pork chops with the bone are your ideal choice as the bone makes for a juicier dish and keeps the meat from shrinking.

1/4 cup fish sauce

1/4 teaspoon chili paste

1 teaspoon sugar

1 tablespoon ground black pepper

4 pork chops (or 2 pounds
   boneless pork)

3 tablespoons oil

2 shallots, diced

1 medium yellow onion, sliced into
   rings

4 cloves garlic, minced

Herb Noodle Salad (see recipe
   in Basics)

1. In a small bowl, combine the fish sauce, chili paste, sugar, and black pepper. Whisk until the sugar is dissolved.

2. Place the pork chops or boneless pork in a shallow dish or bowl or ziplock bag. Pour the marinade all over them, cover the bowl or seal the bag, and leave it in the refrigerator overnight.

3. In a skillet over high heat, warm the oil. Cook the shallots and onion for a few minutes in the hot oil until light brown and fragrant. Add the garlic and cook for another 2 minutes.

4. Add the pork to the skillet and pour any remaining marinade on top. Lower the heat to medium and cook for about 10 minutes on each side or until the surface of the meat has browned and the pork is cooked through.

5. Remove the pork from the heat and let it sit for 15 minutes. Slice the pork chops into bite-size pieces to make it easier for your diners to pick them up and eat them with chopsticks. Arrange the pork pieces over the herb noodle salad and serve with generous amounts of nuoc cham.

[SERVES 4]

Bánh Ướt Thịt

To make this dish, it takes some time to get the hang of creating the thin crepes. But clearly the effort pays off once you've mastered the process. They're like eating light pillows. Probably one of our most nondescript foods, the rice crepe instantly takes on character when filled with this savory ground pork and mushroom mixture, dipped into nuoc cham, and served as a singular main entree or a stunning appetizer.

FILLING:

1/3 cup dried tree ear mushrooms

1 cup warm water

1/2 pound ground pork

2 tablespoons fish sauce

1 tablespoon ground black pepper

1/2 teaspoon sugar

3 cloves garlic, finely chopped

1 shallot, finely chopped

1 tablespoon oil

CREPES (BANH UOT):

2 1/4 cups lukewarm water

1 1/2 cups rice flour

1/4 cup cornstarch

1/3 cup tapioca flour

1/2 tablespoon sugar

1/2 tablespoon salt

1/3 cup oil

1. First make the filling. In a small bowl, reconstitute the mushrooms by placing them in the cup of warm water for 1 hour. In the meantime, in a medium bowl, combine the ground pork, fish sauce, black pepper, sugar, garlic, and shallot. Mix well.

2. When the dried mushrooms are reconstituted, add 1 tablespoon of the liquid from the bowl to the ground pork mixture; mix well. Drain and discard the remaining water from the mushrooms. Finely chop the mushrooms and add them to the ground pork mixture and blend again.

3. Heat the tablespoon of oil in a skillet over medium heat. Sauté the ground pork mixture for about 10 minutes or until it is completely brown. Set it aside in a bowl or a plate.

4. Next, make the rice crepes. Pour the lukewarm water into a bowl. With a wooden spoon or chopsticks, add the rice flour a bit at a time while stirring, making sure to break up any flour lumps. Add the cornstarch, a little at a time. Continue the same process with the tapioca flour. Add the sugar and salt and stir until they are dissolved. Set aside for a half hour.

5. Heat a medium-size, nonstick skillet on a low burner. Lightly brush the skillet with the olive oil. You do not want to fry these crepes, so use the oil sparingly.

6. Pour in about 1/4 cup of the batter, and swirl the skillet around so that the batter evenly spreads. The rice crepe needs to be very thin, like a French crepe and not a pancake. The thinner and the more delicate, the better. Cover the skillet tightly, and let it sit on the burner, still on low heat, for about 3 minutes. Do not let the crepe burn. When done, the crepe will be white and the surface should be dry to the touch.

7. Remove the lid and gently remove the crepe by scraping and loosening the sides first. Place the crepe onto an oiled plate or nonstick baking sheet to cool. Continue making crepes until the batter is gone, making sure to re-oil the skillet between crepes. Do not pile the crepes on top of one another—they are slick and delicate and will stick together.

8. To fill the crepes: Take one crepe at a time and place it on a nonstick surface, such as an oiled plate or oiled baking sheet. Place 2 tablespoons of the pork filling in a thin horizontal line all the way across the bottom third of the crepe. Fold in the sides of the crepe about an inch. Start from the bottom and fold up. The rolled crepe should be about 1 to 1 1/2 inches thick. Set aside and repeat these steps until all the crepes are filled.

9. Crepes can be served hot or at room temperature, individually or family style. Serve with a salad platter and fresh bean sprouts. Garnish with fried scallions, garlic, or unsalted dry-roasted peanuts if you wish. Serve with plenty of nuoc cham.

[SERVES 6 AS AN ENTREE; 8 TO 10 AS AN APPETIZER]

GRILLED PORK CHOPS WITH LEMONGRASS AND GARLIC
Sườn Heo Ướp Xã Tỏi

The aromatic flavors of lemongrass and garlic permeate the pork chops, producing a fragrant dish that is a wonderful complement to a vegetable sauté or a noodle side dish, as well as being delicious with plain steamed rice and the salad platter. If you do not have enough time for the pork chops to marinate at least an hour, you can add another tablespoon of fish sauce.

1 stalk fresh lemongrass, very
   finely chopped

1/2 tablespoon sugar

1/2 teaspoon chili paste

1 medium onion, sliced into rings

6 cloves garlic, minced

1/2 tablespoon fresh lime juice

1/4 cup fish sauce

3 pounds pork chops (or substitute another cut of pork)

1/4 cup vegetable oil

Black pepper to taste

1. In a medium-size mixing bowl, combine the lemongrass, sugar, chili paste, onions, garlic, and lime juice. Mix thoroughly, then add the fish sauce and mix until the sugar has dissolved.

2. In a shallow dish or bowl, arrange the pork chops so that as much of the surface area is exposed as possible. Pour the marinade all over the chops. Cover and refrigerate for at least an hour, but ideally overnight.

3. In a grilling pan, heat the oil over medium heat. Grill the pork chops roughly 10 minutes on each side or until cooked through. Add black pepper to taste. Cut the meat into bite-size pieces so it is easy to pick up with chopsticks. Serve over white rice with a side of nuoc cham and a salad platter.

[SERVES 4]

Restaurants outside the Little Saigon community are about 50 to 75 percent more expensive than those in Little Saigon. Many wonder how long Little Saigon's low prices can last. As the Vietnamese people have prospered, they can afford to pay more, but they certainly do not want to. Such issues remain in debate, as the Vietnamese community questions how to approach tourism and build business for the future.

TRADITIONAL VIETNAMESE SPRING ROLLS WITH PORK, SHRIMP, AND MINT LEAVES

Gỏi Cuốn

Vietnamese spring rolls seem to be hot items in restaurants right now. It's just too bad that people feel they have to go out and pay several dollars for each spring roll when they can easily make them at home for much less. This recipe is for the traditional spring roll—lettuce, herbs wrapped around pork, and shrimp. Once you get the idea, you can make it your own with chicken, shrimp, tofu—whatever suits you. Though a simple dish, its allure comes from the use of rice paper, or banh trang. Not only is rice paper a pliable vehicle for holding ingredients, but it also has a chewy texture and pleasant but subtle salt taste. The great thing about these spring rolls is that they can be made hours ahead of time and kept fresh in the fridge by being wrapped in a damp paper towel. Spring rolls look intricate, but they are easy to assemble. Just remember to keep pressing firmly as you make them.

1/2 pound pork loin with fat and rind, or lean pork meat

3 tablespoons salt

1/2 pound medium fresh shrimp

1 large cucumber

1 head iceberg lettuce

3/4 cup fresh mung bean sprouts

1 cup fresh mint leaves

12 scallions or Chinese chives

1 1/2 cups cooked rice vermicelli (bun)

8 rice paper sheets (the 2 extras are for practice or if a sheet tears)

Peanut Sauce (see recipe in Basics)

1. Pour enough water in a large pot to cover the entire piece of pork. Add the pork and 2 tablespoons of the salt. Cook the pork until it is entirely done (it should not be pink), about 15 minutes, on high heat. Remove the pork from the pot and let it cool.

2. In another saucepan, boil the shrimp with the remaining tablespoon of salt in enough water to cover them. When the shrimp are done, peel and devein them, then slice them lengthwise. Set the shrimp on a plate or in a bowl.

3. When the pork has cooled, slice it against the grain into thin pieces, each roughly 2 by 1 inches in size. Each thin slice should have a piece of lean meat, fat, and rind. Place the pork on a plate or in a bowl.

4. Wash and peel the cucumber, remove the core, and julienne it into 3-inch lengths. Wash the lettuce and shred it with a mandoline or slice it into fine shreds. Measure 1 1/2 cups of shredded lettuce. Wash the bean sprouts and mint leaves. Wash the scallions or chives and trim the ends so that the stalks are about 5 inches in length. Set each of these ingredients aside on separate plates or in bowls.

5. Cut the cooked vermicelli into 3½-inch lengths. Set aside.

6. To begin assembling the spring rolls, you should have all the ingredients close at hand on plates or in bowls.

7. Fill a large bowl with lukewarm water. Submerge a piece of rice paper for about 2 seconds, just enough to make it soft and pliable. If it's too dry, it will easily crack. If it's too wet, it will be too delicate and will tear. When the rice paper is the right consistency, place it in front of you on a wooden board or any flat, nonstick surface.

8. The idea is to build a log of food to be wrapped tightly. Think of dividing all the items into six servings, so begin by placing a sixth of the noodles in a log shape across the bottom third of the rice paper circle. Then add the lettuce, cucumber, bean sprouts, and mint leaves. On top of this, place the sliced pork and then the shrimp. Finally, add 2 scallions or chive stems. To wrap, begin by folding in the left and right sides tightly. Next, fold up the bottom third, and roll tightly into an egg roll shape. The diameter of the spring roll should be about 1 to 1½ inches, depending how much you decided to pile on, or how tight you've rolled the spring roll. Set aside the prepared spring roll on a plate and repeat the process with the other spring rolls.

9. Serve cold or at room temperature with a salad platter, wrapping the herbs around the spring roll and dipping it into the peanut dipping sauce before taking each bite.

[SERVES 6]

FRIED SPRING ROLLS WITH GROUND PORK, FRESH CRAB, AND TREE EAR MUSHROOMS

Chả Giò

Vietnamese fried spring rolls are different from those of other Asian cultures because of their filling (lean pork, crab, shrimp, and mushrooms); the crisper and thinner rice paper used instead of the Asian egg roll wrapper; and the light frying method instead of the deep-frying used for Asian egg rolls. In addition, they are distinctive because they should be eaten with a handful of lettuce and fresh herbs wrapped around them, and they are dipped into nuoc cham (dipping sauce) before each bite. The crunch of the egg rolls and lettuce and the chewiness of the tree ear mushrooms make for an interesting textural contrast. Sometimes we like to wrap cool rice vermicelli (bun) around these crispy fried spring rolls. You can prepare the spring rolls ahead and fry them right before serving.

1 cup (2-inch-long) cooked cellophane noodles (mien)

3/4 pound ground pork butt

1 large yellow onion, finely diced

3 tablespoons finely chopped tree ear mushrooms

4 cloves garlic, minced

2 shallots, finely chopped

1/2 cup fresh crabmeat, preferably from the crab body

1 teaspoon ground black pepper

2 tablespoons fish sauce

12 sheets rice paper

2 cups oil, either olive oil for health and neutral flavoring, or peanut oil for crispness

1. In a large bowl, combine all ingredients except the rice paper and oil in no particular order. Make sure the ingredients are blended thoroughly.

2. Fill a large bowl with lukewarm water. Soak each piece of rice paper for about 10 seconds, just enough to make it soft and pliable. If it's too dry, it will crack easily. If it's too wet, it will be too delicate and will tear. When the rice paper is the right consistency, place it in front of you on a wooden board or any flat, nonstick surface.

3. Fold the round rice paper in half, so that the diameter of the semicircle is horizontally toward you. Put about 2 tablespoons of filling on the bottom third of the semicircle, and mold the filling into a cylindrical shape horizontally. Then fold in the left and right sides up to the edges of the filling. Securing tightly, begin to roll from the bottom up (like a burrito). Avoid trapping any air or space, as this will cause the spring roll to fall apart once fried. Make sure you firmly press together the wrapper to seal the filling inside.

4. Continue with the rest of the wrappers and filling until everything has been used. Set aside on a plate until ready to fry.

5. To fry: Pour just half of the oil into a wok or a deep skillet. The spring rolls do not need to be deep-fried, just lightly fried in a thin layer of oil. Heat the oil to 370 degrees. Test the heat of the oil by dropping in a piece of rice paper or onion; it should bubble and fry immediately.

6. Place the spring rolls into the hot oil just a few at a time, depending on the size of the skillet or wok. Do not overcrowd the spring rolls, as you will need to flip them over. Fry until golden brown, approximately 5 to 8 minutes total. Remove and drain on paper towels. Add more oil to the skillet as needed to fry the remaining spring rolls.

7. Serve spring rolls hot with a salad platter and nuoc cham.

[SERVES 4]

SWEET-AND-SOUR CATFISH SOUP IN PINEAPPLE BROTH
Canh Chua Cá

Canh chua is the quintessential dish representing the south of Vietnam, specifically the Mekong Delta. Fish would be caught in the delta and then brought home to make various main dishes. The carcass would not go to waste; the fish head, tail, and bones would make a stock. Canh chua usually contains chunks of fish, but the fish needs to have a tough, chewy texture, as catfish and monkfish do. It is traditional to serve the soup with the fish bones, tail, and head, but if you think that will be unappealing to your diners, simply remove these parts before serving. My great-aunt tells me that the best way to make this stock is with unsweetened pineapple juice to counter and balance the strong smell of the fish. A vegetarian version of this soup is canh chua chay (see recipe in the Vegetarian Dishes chapter), but it won't have the same brininess and umami as a fish stock made from scratch.

5 cups unsweetened pineapple juice

3 cups water

1 whole catfish carcass (what was once a 1½- to 2-pound fish)

1 1-inch cross-sectional slice catfish, with skin and bones intact

½ tablespoon ground black pepper

1 cup taro stem, sliced into ½-inch pieces

¼ cup fish sauce

1 fresh Thai bird chile, finely chopped

2 tomatoes, each cut into 6 pieces

⅓ cup (½-inch-sliced) fresh okra

⅓ cup diced fresh or canned pineapple

1 cup fresh mung bean sprouts

Fresh cilantro leaves

3 scallions, chopped into rings

1. In a large stockpot, combine the pineapple juice and water and bring to a boil.

2. Clean the catfish carcass, then put it into the pot.

3. Add the slice of fish, black pepper, taro stem, fish sauce, and chopped chile. Lower the heat and let it simmer for 20 minutes.

4. Stir in the tomatoes, okra, pineapple, and bean sprouts. Cook over low heat for 15 minutes.

5. Garnish with fresh cilantro and scallions. Serve with steamed rice or noodles.

[SERVES 4]

SHRIMP BROCHETTES
Bánh Mì Tom Chiên

Lightly fried, the combination of shrimp with the fresh ingredients turns out a nice, full-flavored teaser before your real meal begins. Fresh shrimp is naturally sweet; when it is blended with fragrant onions, garlic, and shallots, it becomes a complex dish that's made even richer when deep-fried. Shrimp brochettes are not as popular as they should be, but I'm seeing more of them in the restaurants in Little Saigon. For a bit of an Americanized twist, these brochettes are now being made with cheese, which I have decided to do here. A stale baguette is the perfect bread to use.

3 cloves garlic, minced

2 shallots

¹⁄₄ onion, roughly chopped

3 tablespoons fish sauce

¹⁄₃ cup plus 1 tablespoon oil

¹⁄₂ pound fresh shrimp or prawns, peeled and deveined

1 teaspoon sugar

¹⁄₂ teaspoon ground black pepper

1 scallion, finely chopped

¹⁄₂ tablespoon rice flour

1 egg plus 1 egg yolk

¹⁄₄ cup finely grated mild white cheese (any kind; optional)

1 baguette

1. Put the garlic, shallots, and onion in a large food processor. Pulse until minced. Add the fish sauce, 1 tablespoon of oil, and the shrimp and continue pulsing until a paste is formed. Transfer the shrimp paste to a medium bowl.

2. To the bowl, add the sugar, black pepper, scallion, rice flour, and eggs. Mix until thoroughly blended. Add the optional grated cheese and mix. Set aside.

3. Slice the baguette into 1-inch slices. Put the slices on one or more baking sheets.

4. Spread a thin layer of the shrimp paste over one side of each baguette slice. The paste should cover the bread slice completely—approximately 1 tablespoon per slice of a standard, narrow baguette.

5. In a large skillet, heat about half of the remaining oil until hot. Place each brochette into the hot oil with the shrimp paste-side down; avoid overcrowding the pan. Cook for about 1 to 3 minutes or until the shrimp side is a golden, pinkish brown. Check by gently lifting and looking at the underside of the brochette while it is frying. Flip the brochette over and fry the other side. Remove the brochettes from the skillet and drain on paper towels. Repeat until all the brochettes have been fried.

6. Serve hot with nuoc cham.

[SERVES 8 AS AN APPETIZER]

Chạo Tom

Shrimp skewers are a simple treat that have become a Vietnamese family standard. There are many different variations, however, which have evolved through the generations of each family. Here's my family's version. The shrimp paste is irresistible when wrapped in lettuce and herbs and dipped into nuoc cham. The sugarcane skewers are deliciously flavored by the shrimp and seasonings and are great for chomping after you've consumed the shrimp paste.

5 tablespoons melted pork or bacon fat (or vegetable shortening such as Crisco)

8 cloves garlic

1 small shallot

1 pound fresh shrimp, peeled and deveined

1 tablespoon fish sauce

1 teaspoon ground black pepper

1 teaspoon sugar

1/4 teaspoon salt

2 tablespoons rice flour

8 pieces fresh sugarcane

1/4 cup oil

1. In a skillet over high heat, melt the pork or bacon fat. If you have to use salted bacon, omit the salt from the shrimp paste. Set the fat aside to cool before adding it to the shrimp paste. (If you're using vegetable shortening, you can skip this step.)

2. In a food processor, mince the garlic and shallots. Set aside in a large bowl.

3. In the same processor, grind the shrimp with the fish sauce until it is completely processed into a paste. Add the shrimp paste to the garlic and shallots. Add the black pepper, sugar, salt, and rice flour. Blend together with a wooden spoon.

4. Add the cooled, softened solid pork fat (or vegetable shortening) to the fish paste and blend in completely. Refrigerate for a half hour so the paste cools and stiffens. The addition of the fat will make the shrimp paste congeal and hold its shape around the skewers.

5. Cut the sugarcane pieces into 5-inch lengths. They should be approximately 1/2 inch wide, the girth of five or six standard stick skewers.

6. Wipe or spray a large baking sheet with vegetable or olive oil. The sheet should be well oiled so the shrimp paste does not stick.

7. Once the shrimp paste has cooled, wash and dry your hands. Scoop about 6 tablespoons of the paste into your hands and wrap the paste around a skewer in an oblong, rough shape, leaving about $3/4$ inch uncovered on each end. Place the skewer on the oiled baking sheet. Continue shaping the paste around the skewers until all the paste is used.

8. To cook the shrimp, begin by preparing a steamer. Make sure the bottom of the steamer is well oiled so the shrimp paste does not stick. Place the skewers in the steamer, providing some space between them. Do not pile them on top of one another. Steam the skewers for about 5 minutes, or until the shrimp paste turns pink. Remove the skewers and set aside. If you wish, you can freeze the shrimp skewers at this point. They will need to be defrosted before you grill them.

9. When you're ready to eat, grill the shrimp skewers until they are slightly charred. Or you can slightly fry the shrimp skewers in light oil in a hot skillet.

10. Serve as a meal over bun or steamed rice, a salad platter, and nuoc cham. As an appetizer, serve with just nuoc cham.

[SERVES 4 AS AN ENTREE OR 8 AS AN APPETIZER]

VERMICELLI SQUARES WITH SCALLION OIL
Bánh Hỏi

Banh hoi vermicelli is specifically used for these squares (which are also known simply as banh hoi). You can substitute them for bun, the herb noodle salad. Wrap the squares with fresh herbs from the salad platter around grilled meats and seafood. They are delicious when they are dipped in fish sauce.

½ pound thin rice vermicelli

½ cup scallion oil (see recipe in Basics)

⅓ cup fried shallots or fried garlic (see recipe in Basics)

1. Soak the rice vermicelli in warm water for 10 minutes.

2. Drain the noodles. Arrange them into a thin (approximately ½ inch thick) flat layer over a cheesecloth or well-oiled plate and place it in a steamer. Cover and steam for about 5 to 10 minutes over medium heat, or until the noodles are stuck together.

3. Remove the noodles from the steamer, keeping them stuck together in one layer. Set aside to cool to room temperature, then cut into approximately 3x3-inch squares. They can also be 3x6-inch squares, folded in half.

4. Drizzle each square with the scallion oil. Stack the squares on a serving plate and top with the fried shallots or fried garlic. Serve with the salad platter, in lieu of an herb noodle salad.

[SERVES 4]

Noodle Soups

PHỞ, HŨ TIEU, AND MI HOUSES

Soup is regarded by some people as a prelude to a much larger meal, a teaser before the real eating begins. But the Vietnamese embrace the idea of having an entire meal in just one single bowl of soup. Some of the most celebrated Vietnamese dishes are soups made of long rice or egg noodles, served in rich beef, pork, or chicken broths. Pho, pronounced fuh, is the most popular of these. The Chinese-style soups of hu tieu and mi complete the triumvirate of Vietnamese noodle soups. Not only are these three types of soups a quintessential part of Vietnamese cuisine, but they are also fresh, nutritious, and cheap—a bowl of pho in Little Saigon still averages $4.00.

In this country pho, hu tieu, and mi houses outnumber any other type of Vietnamese restaurant. In fact, some of the first Vietnamese business establishments were pho houses, opened before the Vietnamese even established Little Saigon. Pho houses can be found in every major city in the world, with more than a hundred in Southern California alone. In Little Saigon it is impossible to walk from one block to another without seeing a pho, hu tieu, or mi establishment. Most of the venerable favorites are concentrated on Bolsa Avenue, Westminster Boulevard, and Brookhurst Avenue.

Popular noodle houses often have lines out the door at breakfast and lunchtime (they're not so crowded at dinner). The atmosphere is always casual, with minimal decor. Napkins, chopsticks, and big plastic soup spoons stay in the center of the tables, in addition to condiments such as Sriracha chili paste, hoisin sauce, vinegar, whole Thai bird chiles or chopped jalapeños, and fish sauce.

The soups served in the Little Saigon noodle houses vary in types of broths, noodles, herbs, textures, and presentation. They also vary from one noodle house to another. For instance, some cooks prefer sweeter broths, while others make spicier broths. The locals know exactly where to go to satisfy a craving for a specific type of noodle soup, such as bun rieu or banh canh gio heo. One popular pho house is rumored to simmer the beef bones for three days, giving the broth its deep brown color. A hu tieu house right off Bolsa Avenue is known for its spectacular hu tieu, but if you come at the right hour (late afternoon), you can have a bowl of the stock bones for free (many enjoy savoring the melt-in-your-mouth meat that falls off the bones as well as the succulent marrow).

Eating noodle soup is a performance in itself. Each table provides just enough elbow room for slurping. Your head is perched just inches above the bowl. Your elbows are out as your hands alternate between wadding up noodles with chopsticks in one hand and sipping broth from the spoon in the other. You tear up herbs from the salad platter by hand and add them directly to the soup.

In this chapter you'll find a variety of soup recipes, all of which mirror what you'll find on a menu at any pho, hu tieu, or mi house in Little Saigon. Asian grocers now sell ready-made seasoning packets to make pho; however, I prefer to make pho from scratch, giving me the ability to control the spice blend. Try using different noodles, different broths, different garnishes. You'll learn to appreciate how noodle size, shape, and texture work together, and as a result you'll learn to create your very own Vietnamese noodle soup recipe.

A few important points to remember about making pho:

- These are slow-cooked broths. They should be allowed to simmer slowly, for hours, at the back of the stove before being served hot, straight into individual serving bowls. Pho ga requires less cooking time than pho bo.
- My aunt Minh tells me she likes to make pho with both chicken and beef bones because beef bones make for a rich broth, while chicken bones sweeten it.
- The charred onion and ginger play a crucial role in adding to the fragrance of the broth. Don't ignore the charring step.
- Be sure to wrap the spices in cheesecloth, or a large mesh tea leaf strainer—which I prefer.
- When pho broth is fully cooked, it should run clear, so keep a fine strainer handy to help clear the broth.

Pho originated in Hanoi, and each region of Vietnam has its own slight variation on the soup. It is said that the broths get sweeter and sweeter as you travel south through Vietnam. Pho from northern Vietnam is not served with any herbs and is not made with fish sauce. You will find this on the menu as pho bac (pho from the North). The people in the city of Hue in Central Vietnam like to make their pho broth a little bit spicier and a tad sweeter. In the South, where pho broth is the sweetest, it is made with fish sauce and served with plenty of herbs on a platter.

Phở Bò

Pho bo, the most popular pho, is more than just a simple beef consommé. The aroma is captivating and the taste is a deliberate collision of salty, sweet, and umami all in one. The Vietnamese learn to appreciate pho by understanding its methodical, complex preparation. Derived from beef bones and cooked with aromatic spices such as cinnamon, star anise, coriander, roasted onion, garlic, and ginger, a pho broth is clear with a deep, multilayered aroma and taste. The intense, boiling broth is then added to servings of mounds of slippery rice noodles and paper-thin slices of rare eye-round beef that immediately cook in the broth. Do be sure to use the oxtail. After being cooked in the broth, it is deliciously flavored and tender. The anise seeds and pods are essential, too. They give the stock a nuttier and slightly smoky flavor. To enhance the finished dish, well-done flank, brisket, tendon, or tripe are sometimes added as well.

3 pounds beef knuckles or neck bones, with meat

2 pounds beef oxtail

10 cups water (or enough to entirely cover meat)

3 large yellow onions, peeled

1 gingerroot, 1/2 size of small palm, roughly peeled

4 whole star anise, with pods

1/2 tablespoon whole cloves

1 tablespoon black peppercorns

4 cloves garlic, smashed

1 daikon, peeled and cut into 3 pieces

1 cinnamon stick

3 small shallots

1/2 cup rock sugar, roughly palm size

1 cup fish sauce

2 tablespoons salt

2 6-ounce packages flat rice noodles (pho)

3/4 pound sirloin or top round steak, sliced paper-thin

6 scallions, chopped into rings

PHO SALAD PLATTER:

Sriracha chili sauce

Hoisin sauce

Fresh cilantro leaves

Green limes, quartered

Fresh mung bean sprouts

Fresh Thai basil leaves

Fresh perilla leaves

Fresh long coriander leaves

Fresh whole red or green chiles

1. Put the beef knuckles or bones and oxtail in a very large stockpot, and cover completely with water. Bring to a boil and keep boiling while you prepare the rest of the ingredients.

2. Cut two peeled yellow onions in half. Char each onion half by holding it with tongs over the open flame of the gas stove or place it directly on the electric burner for about 3 minutes. You do not need to light the onion on fire, but the charring will bring out the aroma and deepen the flavor of the broth. Repeat the process with the ginger. Putting the onion or ginger under a broiler will also work. Set aside.

3. In a small skillet or saucepan, lightly toast the anise pods, cloves, peppercorns, and garlic for about 5 minutes, or until fragrant. Set aside to cool. Then wrap them in a piece of cheesecloth or put them in a spice bag or tea strainer.

4. Check on the bones in the stockpot and skim off any scum that has accumulated. (If this is your first time making a beef stock from scratch, you may be surprised by the amount of scum that builds up from the meat. It's important to skim the top of the simmering broth in the first few hours of cooking.)

5. Add the spice bag, charred onion and ginger, daikon, cinnamon stick, and shallots to the stock. Boil for 15 minutes, and then bring down to a simmer.

6. Add the rock sugar, fish sauce, and salt, and stir well. Continue to simmer for $2^{1}/_{2}$ hours, uncovered. Check the pot periodically and skim off any scum or fat as it accumulates.

7. Though the broth will be flavorful after $2^{1}/_{2}$ hours and you may think it's done, continue cooking on very low heat for up to 10 hours, covered. The broth will only get better.

8. Once the broth has finished cooking, remove the pot from the heat and let it cool a bit. Then remove all the solid ingredients from the broth. Do not discard the bones; set them aside to remove any meat remaining on them. Pour the broth through a fine mesh strainer to remove any scum and fat, then return the broth to the pot or a new pot. The broth should be clear.

[CONTINUED ON NEXT PAGE]

9. About 15 minutes before you would like to serve the pho, bring the broth back to a boil. While you are reboiling, fill a large bowl with hot tap water. Soak the rice noodles in the water for about 10 minutes. They should soften just slightly; the hot pho broth will cook them the rest of the way.

10. Drain the noodles and place them in six individual serving bowls. Slice the beef paper-thin against the grain, if your butcher has not done so. With your sharpest, thin-blade knife, try your best to slice paper-thin pieces. If the meat is very cold (even slightly frozen), it is easier to handle and to slice.

11. Slice the remaining onion paper-thin, preferably with a mandoline. Arrange the raw beef and onion slices and scallions over the noodles in each bowl. Slice the oxtail and add it to the noodles as well, in addition to any of the bits of meat taken from the bones.

12. When ready to serve, pour the boiling broth into the individual bowls. The broth will cook the beef as well as the noodles. Give it a few minutes to do so, then serve with the pho garnish platter. The herbs should be separated into their groups, not mixed together. Encourage your diners to take some fresh herbs, tear them with their hands, and throw them into the broth. A light squeeze of lime cuts the richness of the broth a bit. The hoisin sauce and Sriracha chili sauce can be added directly to the soup or poured into a side dish as a dip for the beef.

[SERVES 6]

One of the best hu tieu houses in Little Saigon is the tiny Trieu Chau, located on the corner of Bolsa Avenue and Newhope Street. It always has a line out the door. Trieu Chau has been around since Little Saigon started and remains a fine establishment for those wanting the very best in hu tieu or mi soups.

CHICKEN PHO
Phở Gà

Chicken pho is just as satisfying as beef pho, but it invigorates your palate in a different way—chicken pho has the zing of lemongrass but lacks the woody, spiced fragrance of the cinnamon and star anise found in beef pho. Chicken pho tends to be more commonly made at home, as the stock can be made with the chicken bones from a prior evening's meal. Like most of the world, the Vietnamese think chicken soup is great to have when sick, but it is the lemongrass that many believe provides the curative element. Most pho restaurants serve mostly beef pho and that's usually what's ordered, but there is one chicken pho restaurant hidden off Ward Street that is famous for serving the best chicken broth in the town. The restaurant even has a chicken pho for which you can request the addition of chicken embryos.

3 pounds chicken and bones, skinless

Water for stock

3 large yellow onions, peeled

1 gingerroot (size of a small palm),
   roughly peeled

1 large daikon, peeled and cut into
   3 large pieces

2 stalks fresh lemongrass, outer layers
   removed

3 shallots, peeled

3 whole cloves

1 tablespoon black peppercorns

4 cloves garlic, smashed

1/3 cup fish sauce

1 medium piece rock sugar (1/3 size of a palm),
   or 1/4 cup granulated sugar

1/2 tablespoon salt

2 6-ounce packages flat rice noodles (pho)

6 scallions, chopped into rings

PHO SALAD PLATTER:

Ginger dipping sauce

Sriracha chili sauce

Hoisin sauce

Fresh cilantro leaves

Green limes, quartered

Fresh mung bean sprouts

Fresh Thai basil leaves

Fresh perilla leaves

Fresh long coriander leaves

Fresh red or green chiles, chopped

[CONTINUED ON NEXT PAGE]

1. Put chicken and bones in a very large stockpot, and cover completely with water. Bring to a boil and keep boiling while you prepare the rest of the ingredients.

2. Cut two of the peeled yellow onions in half. Char each onion half by holding it with tongs over the open flame of the gas stove or place it directly on the electric burner. Keep it in the flame for about 3 minutes. You do not need to light the onion on fire, but putting it to a flame or electric burner will bring out the aromas. Repeat the process to char the ginger. Putting the onion or the ginger under a broiler can also work. Set aside.

3. Add the daikon, lemongrass stalks, and shallots to the stock.

4. In a skillet, lightly toast the cloves, peppercorns, and garlic for about 5 minutes, or until fragrant. Set aside and let cool. Then wrap them in a piece of cheesecloth or put them in a spice bag or tea strainer.

5. Skim off any scum in the stockpot. Add the spice bag, fish sauce, rock sugar, and salt to the pot. Continue boiling for another 15 minutes, and then lower the heat to a simmer. Continue cooking for 3 1/2 hours, uncovered. Check the pot periodically and skim off any scum and fat as it is produced.

6. Remove the pot from the heat and let the broth cool.

7. Remove all the contents from the cooled broth and discard everything but the chicken. Pour the broth through a fine strainer to remove any scum or fat, and return the broth to the pot. It should be clear.

8. About 15 minutes before you would like to serve pho, bring the broth back to a boil.

9. Remove the chicken meat from the bones. Cut any large pieces of chicken meat into thin slices. Set the meat aside.

10. Fill a large bowl with hot tap water. Soak the rice noodles in the water for about 10 minutes. They should soften just slightly; the hot broth will cook them the rest of the way. Drain the noodles and put them into six individual serving bowls.

11. Slice the remaining onion paper-thin, preferably with a mandoline.

12. Place the slices of chicken and onion and a handful of scallions over the noodles in each bowl.

13. Just before serving, add the hot broth to the bowls. Present the noodle bowls with the garnish platter. Encourage your diners to take some fresh herbs, tear them with their hands, and throw them into the broth. A light squeeze of lime cuts the richness of the broth a bit. The hoisin sauce and Sriracha chili sauce can be placed directly into the soup or poured in a side dish as a dip for the chicken.

[SERVES 6]

Many theories exist as to the origins of pho. My brother, a biochemist at UCLA, and his Vietnamese classmates believe the Vietnamese wanted to blanch bones for decorative jewelry, and the residual broth from the boiled bones became food broth. A less far-fetched theory is that beef noodle soup first surfaced as a hybrid recipe born of French and Chinese influences in the nineteenth century in Hanoi, and that as people began fleeing the Communists in North Vietnam, they brought pho to the rest of the country. The word pho is said to come from *feu* of *pot au feu* or just plain *feu,* French for "flame." The theory is that this described the flames of the pho street vendors.

EGG NOODLE SOUP WITH DUCK
Mì Vịt Tiêm

Mi, or egg noodles, are wonderful served in rich, concentrated pork broths such as hu tieu. Mi vit tiem is one of the most popular variations served at mi houses in Little Saigon. Like hu tieu, mi is a Chinese-style soup; therefore, it is not served with a salad platter as pho is. Duck—braised, roasted, grilled—is delicious in soups. You can buy your own roasted duck in Little Saigon or even Chinatown, or follow the recipe for Five-spiced Chicken (substituting duck for the chicken) in this book. Additionally, you can substitute shrimp and squid for the duck for a seafood version (mi do bien), or add tofu. For a little variation, try xa xiu pork as a topping. It is a sweetened pork shoulder meat, with a bit of red coloring.

3 pounds pork bones, preferably knuckle
   bones

2 large yellow onions, peeled and halved

1 gingerroot (size of a small palm), roughly
   peeled

1/2 cup dried shrimp

5 shallots, peeled

4 cloves garlic, smashed

1 tablespoon black peppercorns

1 piece rock sugar (1/4 size of a palm), or
   3 1/2 tablespoons granulated sugar

1 1/2 tablespoons salt

10 cups water

1 pound boneless pork loin or another
   lean pork meat

8 cups cooked egg noodles

1 whole roasted duck, cut into 6 parts
   (purchased or homemade; see recipe
   on page 129, substituting duck for chicken)

4 scallions, chopped into rings

1/2 cup fried shallots

Fresh mung bean sprouts

1. Rinse and scrub the pork bones. Put them into a large stockpot.

2. Char each onion half by holding it over an open gas flame with tongs for about 2 minutes or until it is fragrant. You can also place each onion directly on an electric burner. Char the ginger using the same procedure.

3. Add the charred onions and gingerroot, dried shrimp, shallots, garlic, peppercorns, rock sugar, and salt to the stockpot. Fill the pot with the water and turn on the heat to high. Add the pork loin to the pot. Bring the pot to a boil and cook for 30 minutes, uncovered. Lower the heat to a simmer and cook on low for another 2 hours. Remove the scum as it forms on the surface of the broth.

4. Pour the broth through a fine strainer to remove any scum or fat, and return the broth to the pot. It should be clear. Fifteen minutes before serving, bring the broth back to a rolling boil.

5. Divide the noodles into six individual serving bowls. Place a piece of roasted duck over the noodles in each bowl. Add the scallions and fried shallots to each bowl.

6. Pour the hot broth into the bowls and fill them to the top. Serve with fresh mung bean sprouts.

[SERVES 6]

Hũ Tiêu

Hu tieu is a Chinese noodle soup adopted and slightly modified by the Vietnamese people. This rich pork stock serves as the base for mi as well, but the two differ in the type of noodles (mi uses egg noodles; hu tieu uses rice noodles) and toppings used. At a noodle house, hu tieu can vary by accompaniments, such as barbecued pork (thit xa xiu), ground pork, duck, seafood, and even items like liver. Here is a common version of hu tieu incorporating shrimp and pork.

3 pounds pork bones, preferably knuckle
   bones

2 large yellow onions, peeled

1/2 cup dried shrimp

1 large daikon, peeled and cut into 3 large
   pieces

5 shallots, peeled

4 cloves garlic, peeled and smashed

1 tablespoon black peppercorns

1 piece rock sugar (1/4 size of your palm),
   or 3 1/2 tablespoons granulated sugar

10 cups water

1/3 cup plus 1 tablespoon fish sauce

1 teaspoon salt

1 pound boneless pork loin, or another lean
   pork meat

1 1/2 pounds flat rice noodles (hu tieu)

2 tablespoons oil

1/3 pound ground pork

1/2 pound fresh raw shrimp, peeled
   and deveined, tails on

1/2 cup fried shallots

4 scallions, chopped into rings

1 lime, quartered

Fresh cilantro

1 bunch fresh Chinese chives, cut in
   4-inch lengths

Fresh mung bean sprouts

The serving sizes of all noodle soups are small, large, and xe lua, which translates to "train." I'm not sure where the locomotive comparison comes from, but the bowl is certainly enormous and I figure it means either "We're serving you enough to fill a train" or "You'll be so full, you'll want to throw yourself in front of one."

1. Put the pork bones in a large stockpot.

2. Cut the onions in half and, using tongs, place them over the gas flame on your stove for about 2 minutes or until fragrant. You can also place the onions directly on an electric burner for the same amount of time. Add the onions to the pot.

3. Add the dried shrimp, daikon, shallots, garlic, peppercorns, and rock sugar to the stockpot. Fill the pot with 10 cups of water. Add $1/3$ cup of the fish sauce and the salt and stir. Bring to a boil and cook for 30 minutes, uncovered.

4. After 30 minutes, bring the broth down to a simmer for another 2 hours. Remove the scum as it accumulates on the surface of the broth. After $1 1/2$ hours add the pork loin to the broth. Cook the pork loin for 30 minutes, then remove and set aside to cool. Pour the broth through a fine strainer to remove any scum or fat, and return the broth to the pot. It should be clear.

5. Soak the rice noodles in warm to hot water for 15 minutes. Drain the noodles and divide them into six individual serving bowls.

6. Meanwhile, in a skillet, heat the oil and sauté the ground pork with the remaining tablespoon of fish sauce. Cook, stirring, until done. Set aside.

7. After the pork loin has cooled, cut it into thin slices. Divide the slices into six servings and place them over the noodles. Divide the raw shrimp, fried shallots, ground pork, and scallions into six servings and place them over the pork and noodles.

8. Fifteen minutes before serving, bring the stock back to a rolling boil. Pour the hot broth into each bowl. The hot broth will cook the raw shrimp. Serve with limes, cilantro, chives, and bean sprouts as garnishes.

[SERVES 6]

HUE-STYLE HOT AND SPICY BEEF STEW
Bún Bò Huế

Originating in Hue, this soup reflects Central Vietnam's love for hot, spicy foods and lemongrass. The heat of the broth, contrasted with the cool fresh herbs (cilantro and Thai basil) and the tang of lemongrass, creates bright bold tastes and an extraordinary bowl of soup. Use the thickest vermicelli noodle here (bun day), which has the thickness of spaghetti. These noodles are not often used in Asian dishes, which adds to this dish's distinctive taste and texture. Ideally, bun bo Hue includes pork trotters, but if you are averse to pork hocks or pig's feet, you can substitute pork shoulder or another fatty pork cut. My mom's best friend, who is from Hue, says that bun bo hue should not be served with a salad platter. Showing her Hue pride, she says that all the people in Little Saigon from South Vietnam have ruined the dish by adding the salad platter. The only garnish she thinks should be served with soup is banana blossom; even that, however, isn't necessary if you cannot find it. But many restaurants enjoy serving fresh, crisp herbs and lettuce to enhance the broth and provide a cool, refreshing contrast to the heat of the soup.

6 tablespoons vegetable oil

1 large yellow onion, diced

3/4 pound pork hocks

1 pound pork leg/feet

1/2 pound beef round or London broil

2 pounds pork bones with meat

Water for stock

1 tablespoon annatto seeds

4 stalks fresh lemongrass, outer layers
   removed

1 1/2 tablespoons chili powder

1/2 tablespoon salt

1 1/2 tablespoons shrimp paste

1/2 tablespoon sugar

4 tablespoons fish sauce

2 fresh Thai bird chiles, finely chopped

1/2 tablespoon peppercorns

3/4 pound (1 package) thick rice vermicelli (bun day),
   cooked and drained

Additional shrimp paste

SALAD PLATTER:

1 yellow onion, finely sliced with mandoline

2 cups fresh mung bean sprouts

Fresh Thai basil leaves

Fresh cilantro leaves

2 limes, quartered

2 scallions, cut in 3-inch lengths

Thinly sliced banana blossoms

Shredded iceberg lettuce

Fresh perilla leaves

1. Heat ¼ cup oil in a large stockpot over high heat. When hot, add the diced onions and cook for 5 minutes, still on high heat. Add the pork hock, pork leg/feet, and beef round or London broil. Brown all sides for about 15 minutes. Add the pork bones. Fill the pot with water until it covers the meat and bones. Boil on high heat for 30 minutes, uncovered.

2. In a skillet or small saucepan, heat 2 tablespoons of the oil with the annatto seeds. Stir the seeds quickly with the oil until they have completely bled their reddish color into the oil. Add the oil and seeds to the stock.

3. Add the lemongrass, chili powder, salt, shrimp paste, sugar, fish sauce, chiles, and peppercorns to the stock. Stir well. Lower the heat so the stock can simmer for 1½ hours.

4. Periodically skim off any scum and fat from the stock as it accumulates. After 1½ hours of cooking, remove the meat bones from the stock. Strain the stock through a fine-mesh strainer to remove the seeds, lemongrass, and other ingredients.

5. Slice the beef and pork hocks into thin slices against the grain. Divide the cooked rice vermicelli into four individual serving bowls. Place the beef and pork slices over the noodles. Fill the bowls with the hot broth and serve with the salad platter. Put some shrimp paste in a small bowl to serve with the soup.

[SERVES 4]

CHICKEN AND MUSHROOM SOUP WITH CASSAVA NOODLES
Miến Gà

Because cassava noodles (mien) are very chewy in texture and very filling, mien ga should not be served in the same proportion as a bowl of pho. Besides the texture play of cassava noodles and tree ear mushrooms, this soup is sweeter than other Vietnamese chicken soups or canh consommés because of the daikon and carrots. If you do not want to make the chicken stock from scratch, use 8 cups of unsalted chicken broth. Vietnamese coriander gives a nice pungent and bitter bite to the soup. You can't have the soup without it. The acidity of the lime adds a nice and simple zing.

3 pounds skinless whole chicken or
   chicken parts

Water for stock

2 yellow onions, peeled and cut in half

5 cloves garlic, peeled and smashed

1 large daikon, peeled

2 medium carrots, peeled

1 tablespoon sugar

1 teaspoon coriander seeds

1 tablespoon peppercorns

1/4 cup fish sauce

1 teaspoon salt

1/3 cup tree ear mushrooms

1 fresh Thai bird chile, finely chopped

3 cups uncooked cassava noodles

4 scallions, chopped into rings

Ground black pepper

SALAD PLATTER:

1 lime, quartered

Fresh Vietnamese coriander leaves

1. Place the chicken in a large stockpot. Pour in water to completely cover the chicken, approximately 10 cups. Add the onions, garlic, daikon, carrots, sugar, coriander seeds, and peppercorns. Bring to a boil and cook for 30 minutes, uncovered.

2. Add the fish sauce, salt, mushrooms, and chile. Bring to a simmer and cook for another 2 hours, covered.

3. Strain the broth to remove all the contents. Let cool, then remove the chicken meat from the bones. Shred the meat and set it aside.

4. In a large bowl, soak the cassava noodles in cold water for about 20 minutes. The noodles will be long. Cut them into 8-inch lengths and separate them into individual serving bowls. Arrange the shredded chicken on top of the noodles.

5. Fifteen minutes before serving, bring the broth back to a rolling boil. Pour the hot broth into the bowls with the noodles and chicken. Garnish each serving with the scallions and black pepper. Serve with a salad platter with a quartered lime and Vietnamese coriander.

[SERVES 4 TO 6]

CRAB AND PORK HOCK SOUP WITH UDON NOODLES
Bánh Canh Cua Giò Heo

This is one of those gratifying dishes that I love to order at certain restaurants in Little Saigon that I know make a perfect bowl of soup. It's a lovely bowl of thick noodles tangled in succulent crabmeat. Not only does crab add a great taste to the soup, but when it's broken up in the soup it gives a nice texture. Pork hocks are the ankle joints of the pig, usually from the forelegs. If you don't feel like making the pork stock, you can substitute ready-made chicken stock.

10 cups unsalted chicken stock
   (purchased or homemade)

1/2 pound pork hock, cut into cross-
   sectional 1-inch slices (ask your
   butcher), or pork shoulder or loin

1 yellow onion, peeled and halved

2 shallots, peeled and crushed

5 cloves garlic, peeled and crushed

1/4 cup fish sauce

3 tablespoons oil

1 tablespoon black peppercorns

1 1/2 tablespoons sugar

1/2 cup dried shrimp

1 fresh Thai bird chile, finely chopped

1 cup fresh crabmeat

6 cups cooked udon noodles (banh
   canh)

2 scallions, chopped into rings

1/4 cup fried shallots

SALAD PLATTER:

1 lime, quartered

Fresh cilantro leaves

Fresh mung bean sprouts

1. Bring the chicken stock to a boil in a large stockpot. Add the pork, onion halves, shallots, garlic, fish sauce, oil, black peppercorns, sugar, dried shrimp, and chile. Stir until the sugar is dissolved. Boil for about 20 minutes and then reduce to a simmer.

2. Carefully remove the pork from the simmering stock. Let it cool, then roughly chop the pork hock or cut the shoulder or loin into slices. Set aside.

3. Meanwhile, add the crabmeat to the stock and continue simmering for another 30 minutes. Remove the pot from the heat if you are not ready to serve.

4. Fifteen minutes before serving, bring the soup back to a boil. Divide the noodles into four individual serving bowls. Put the pork, scallions, and fried shallots on top of the noodles. Ladle the hot broth on top and serve immediately with the salad platter.

[SERVES 4]

VERMICELLI NOODLE SOUP WITH GROUND CRAB
AND EGG AND TOMATOES
Bún Riêu

The fragrance and acidity of the tomatoes balance out this noodle soup so that the shrimp and crab are not overwhelming. Not every restaurant makes a decent bowl of bun rieu. There are a few Hue-specific restaurants in Little Saigon that specialize in this soup, and it's the only thing any diner will order.

10 cups unsalted chicken stock (homemade
   or purchased)

1/2 cup fish sauce

1/3 cup dried shrimp

1 tablespoon black peppercorns

1/2 tablespoon sugar

3 large ripe tomatoes, quartered

1 tablespoon oil

1 large onion, peeled

2 shallots, peeled

5 cloves garlic, peeled

1 1/2 cups fresh crabmeat

2 1/2 tablespoons shrimp paste

4 large eggs

1/2 teaspoon salt

1/2 teaspoon pepper

1/2 pound thick rice vermicelli (bun day)

4 scallions, chopped into rings

Additional shrimp paste

SALAD PLATTER:

Limes, quartered

Fresh perilla leaves

Fresh Thai basil leaves

Fresh mung bean sprouts

Fresh mint leaves

Fresh cilantro leaves

Many pho restaurants in Little Saigon have double-digit numbers in their names: Pho 54, Pho 75, and so forth. The numbers signify important years for the owners. For example, Pho 54 is named for the year 1954, because of the owner's nostalgia for some of the more peaceful times in Vietnam; Pho 75 might represent the year the family or business owners first arrived in the United States, or the year their first child was born. If you are in a numbered pho restaurant, ask the owner the significance of the year.

1. In a stockpot, bring the chicken stock to a boil. Add the fish sauce, dried shrimp, peppercorns, and sugar, and stir until the sugar is dissolved. Boil for about a half hour. Lower the heat to a simmer and add the tomatoes. Continue simmering, uncovered, for another 15 minutes.

2. Meanwhile, in a small skillet heat oil over medium heat. Sauté the onions and shallots for a few minutes before adding the garlic. Cook for 5 minutes. Add the crabmeat and shrimp paste. Sauté for 8 minutes. Remove from the heat and set aside.

3. In a small bowl, beat the eggs with the salt and pepper until the eggs are light and fluffy. Add the crabmeat mixture to the beaten eggs. Set aside.

4. Slowly pour the egg and crabmeat mixture into the cooking stock. Gently run chopsticks or a fork through the egg mixture to lightly separate the eggs. You want the egg mixture to clump up in the soup. Continue cooking for another 30 minutes over low heat. Remove the pot from the heat if you're not ready to serve.

5. Bring the soup back to a boil 10 minutes before serving.

6. In a small pot, bring water to a boil to cook the vermicelli noodles. Cook noodles for just 3 minutes, drain, and cool with cold water. Divide noodles into six individual serving bowls. Garnish each serving with the scallions.

7. Ladle the hot broth along with chunks of tomato and the egg and crab mixture over the noodles. Serve hot with the salad platter and a bowl of shrimp paste.

[SERVES 6]

Vegetarian Dishes
THE BUDDHIST TEMPLES

For some in the Western world, *vegetarian* automatically implies tasteless, unattractive, low-protein meals. But the Vietnamese, whose culture and cuisine are rooted in Buddhism, know differently. They know how to creatively use ingredients such as bean products, roots, tubers, fungi, grains, and vegetables—all of which first sustained Buddha's followers. The vegetarian diet has been with the Vietnamese for so many centuries that they are recognized for having some of the best vegetarian dishes around. And even though many Vietnamese are not strict vegetarians or vegans, their cuisine focuses on balanced meals with only small portions of meat and seafood dishes along with plenty of fresh vegetables and herbs. Balance, after all, is the essence of Buddhism, along with having a respect for karma and an understanding that everything you do will affect the world around you—people, animals, the environment, and so on.

In a way, Buddhists can be seen as the world's first nutritionists. Buddhist doctrine acknowledges the importance of nutrients and flavors in food. Because nutrients vary from one food item to another, people should eat many different foods instead of only a few. This is certainly reflected in the diverse dishes that can be had at any single Vietnamese meal. Buddhists also believe that it is essential for meals to be focused around all five flavors: Sour nourishes the liver, bitter and pungent nourish the heart, sweet nourishes the spleen, pungent nourishes the lungs, and salty nourishes the spleen and kidneys.

The religion of Buddhism, which was originated in India by Siddhartha Gautama—the Buddha—was introduced to Vietnam by Chinese monks during China's Tang dynasty in the early seventh century. Today more Vietnamese are Buddhists than any other religion. Buddhism is credited with influencing Vietnamese philosophy and ideology, as well as food and diet. The traditions of Buddhism are still evident today in Little Saigon, where there are more than fifty Buddhist temples, monasteries, and worship sanctuaries in a 5-mile area as well as dozens of vegetarian-only restaurants providing exquisite vegetarian meals for both Buddhists and non-Buddhists to enjoy.

Most temples are ranch-style homes in residential neighborhoods that have been transformed into places of worship. These simpler temples have Buddhist and South Vietnamese flags in the front yard with ornate statues like the Buddha in the backyard. There are just a few ornate temples—such as Chua Hue Quang on West Westminster Avenue, the most famous temple in Little Saigon—that exemplify glorious Buddhist art and architecture, with Japanese roof tiles and elaborately landscaped East Asian gardens. Out-of-town Vietnamese always come to visit these magnificent temples, especially on holidays such as Tet.

Though temples primarily serve as a place for individuals to worship and to pray for their deceased loved ones and their families, they are also a center for a variety of other community activities for all generations. Parents bring their children to learn the Vietnamese language, Buddhist doctrine and history, as well as Vietnamese culture. Performances with singing, dancing, and skits are given. A young man will be doing tai chi in the garden next to an elderly man twice his age. Children are in the kitchen helping the elderly ladies cook the vegetarian lunch that will be served to anyone wanting a delicious, home-cooked meal. (The meal is free, but a small donation is suggested.) The temples are particularly busy on certain days of the month (depending on the moon) when Buddhists abstain from meat because of fasting.

The recipes in this chapter are commonly served at any Little Saigon Buddhist temple or vegetarian restaurant. You can create your own recipes by adding or substituting other vegetables and herbs or meat substitutes.

PAN-FRIED TOFU AND BROCCOLI WITH LEMONGRASS AND CHILE
Đậu Hủ Xào Xã Ớt

One of our easiest recipes, this pan-fried tofu and vegetable dish gives you a rudimentary lesson on how to put together basic ingredients and herbs into a healthy, flavorful meal. The multitalented tofu is a fabulous product, not only for its taste but also for the many ways it can be cooked and served. Besides its health benefits, tofu is the perfect food to soak up every flavor it is cooked with. Be careful not to overcook the broccoli; in Vietnamese cuisine, if you are not eating your veggies fresh, you must at least give them a crunch. You may substitute your own favorite vegetables, or even add chicken or beef for a little bit more protein.

12 ounces (1 large or 2 small
   packages) firm tofu

3 cloves garlic, finely chopped

1/2 red or green fresh Thai bird
   chile, finely chopped, with seeds

5 tablespoons fish sauce

1/2 tablespoon sugar

1 small head broccoli

1/4 cup olive oil

1 large yellow onion, sliced in rings

1 stalk fresh lemongrass, cut into
   1 1/2-inch lengths

1/2 tablespoon ground black
   pepper

1/4 cup chopped fresh cilantro
   leaves

1 scallion, chopped into rings

1. Cut the tofu into 1x2-inch rectangles (you can cut it into any shape you like, but the minimum size should be 1-inch cubes).

2. In a separate bowl, combine the garlic, chile and chile seeds, fish sauce, and sugar.

3. Wash and separate the broccoli and chop into individual florets. You will need 2 cups of broccoli.

4. In a large skillet, heat the olive oil over medium heat. When hot, add the tofu and onion rings and cook for a few minutes. Add the broccoli florets, fish sauce mixture, and lemongrass. Pan-fry for about 8 minutes, until the tofu has browned on all sides and the broccoli is cooked.

5. Transfer the tofu and broccoli to a serving bowl with the juices from the pan.

6. Garnish with the black pepper, cilantro, and scallions. Serve with steamed rice or rice vermicelli.

[SERVES 3]

WIDE RICE NOODLES STIR-FRIED WITH TOFU AND VEGETABLES
Bún Xào Chay

Oriental stir-fry noodle dishes are always heavy and delicious because of the amount of oil and fat that goes into their preparation. Vietnamese noodle stir-fries, however, use very little oil. Instead, fish sauce, Maggi sauce, and the juices of the cooked vegetables are used. Not only is this a healthier alternative, it is also much tastier.

1 8-ounce package thick rice noodles (pho or hu tieu noodles)

1/4 cup fish sauce

1/2 tablespoon sugar

1/2 tablespoon black pepper

2 scallions, chopped into rings

1 1/2 tablespoons hoisin sauce

1 tablespoon Maggi Seasoning Sauce

3 tablespoons oil

1/2 onion, sliced into rings

1 large shallot, diced

5 cloves garlic, finely chopped

1/2 fresh Thai bird chile, finely chopped

1 cup roughly chopped fresh broccoli

1/2 cup peeled and shredded carrots

1/2 cup snow peas

1/2 cup fresh mung bean sprouts

1/2 cup canned straw mushrooms

1 cup (1 1/2-inch cubes) tofu

1/4 cup chopped fresh mint leaves

1/4 cup chopped fresh cilantro leaves

1. Fill a large pot with water and bring the water to a rolling boil. Turn off the heat and add the rice noodles to the pot. Let them sit in the water for just a few minutes to "cook," and then drain them in a colander. You will need 3 cups of cooked noodles.

2. In a small bowl, whisk together the fish sauce, sugar, black pepper, scallions, hoisin sauce, and Maggi sauce until the sugar is dissolved. Set aside.

3. In a large skillet or wok, heat the oil for about 3 minutes. Begin by cooking the onions and shallots for about 3 minutes. Then add the garlic and chile and cook for another 5 minutes.

4. Add the broccoli and carrots and cook for a few minutes. When they are slightly soft, add the snow peas, bean sprouts, straw mushrooms, and tofu. Sauté and toss frequently as the vegetables and tofu cook for another few minutes.

5. Toss in the fish sauce mixture when you see the vegetables and tofu are close to being done. Make sure all the vegetables and tofu are well coated with the fish sauce mixture.

6. Add the rice noodles and toss everything together, making sure all the vegetables and noodles are evenly blended.

7. Garnish with the mint and cilantro and serve directly from the skillet or wok as a side or main dish.

[SERVES 4 TO 6]

VEGETABLES AND TOFU SAUTEED IN OYSTER SAUCE
Rau Cải Đậu Hủ Xào

This dish is a fine example of the vegetarian, or chay, dishes available at Little Saigon restaurants and Buddhist temples. Rich in vegetable goodness, it is often served with rice or noodles to soak up the sauce. The tofu adds a nice, meaty texture. This is one of those great recipes where you can create a number of variations by adding or substituting some vegetables, seafood, or meat, but it's the blend of shallots, garlic, oyster sauce, sugar, and black pepper that needs to stay intact. Oyster sauce is both sweet and salty, blending evenly with the flavors of the vegetables.

1 large Asian eggplant, peeled and
  cut into 1-inch-thick slices

3 tablespoons salt

3 tablespoons oil

2 shallots, diced

5 cloves garlic, finely chopped

1 cup fresh snow peas

2 cups fresh Vietnamese water
  spinach

1/4 cup oyster sauce

1/2 teaspoon sugar

3 tablespoons fish sauce

12 ounces (1 large or 2 small
  packages) firm tofu, diced
  into 1-inch cubes

1 scallion, chopped into rings

1/2 teaspoon ground black pepper

1/2 cup fresh mung bean sprouts

1. Disperse the eggplant pieces over a baking sheet. Sprinkle them with 3 tablespoons of the salt, and let sit for 20 minutes to sweat out the bitterness.

2. In a large skillet, heat the olive oil. Over medium to high heat, sauté the shallots for a few minutes. Add the garlic and cook for another 3 minutes.

3. Rinse the salt from the eggplant pieces, pat them dry, and add them to the skillet. Cook for 15 minutes or until the eggplant is extremely tender.

4. Add the snow peas, water spinach, and oyster sauce. Stir well. Sprinkle the sugar and fish sauce over the vegetables and stir. Cook for 8 minutes and then add the tofu and scallions. Cook for another 5 minutes or until the tofu is soft.

5. Put on a large platter and garnish with the black pepper and bean sprouts. Serve hot with steamed rice or egg noodles.

[SERVES 4]

SAUTEED BOK CHOY WITH TOFU AND HOISIN SAUCE
Cải Bẹ Trắng Xào

Sautéed bok choy with some tofu and hoisin sauce is delicious and simple to make. Try it with any other vegetables you have around the house.

2 tablespoons oil

1/2 onion, sliced

3 garlic cloves, chopped

1/4 cup hoisin sauce

3 tablespoons fish sauce

1/2 teaspoon salt

1/2 tablespoon sugar

1 teaspoon ground black pepper

4 cups roughly chopped bok choy

2 cups 1/2-inch cubed tofu

1. In a skillet, heat the oil over medium heat. Add the onions and garlic and sauté for 5 minutes.

2. In a small bowl, combine the hoisin sauce, fish sauce, salt, sugar, and pepper.

3. Add the bok choy and tofu to the skillet and toss in the hoisin sauce mixture. Continue sautéing for about 5 minutes until the bok choy has wilted. Serve immediately with steamed rice.

[SERVES 4]

The Vietnamese traditionally pay great reverence to the graves and markers of their loved ones. Because of their belief that our ancestors are always with us, you'll find burning incense, flowers, pinwheels, fruit, and even a tape recorder with Buddhist chanting at grave sites in any Vietnamese cemetery.

SAUTEED MUSTARD GREENS WITH OYSTER SAUCE
Cải Tàu Xào Dầu Hau

Mustard greens are resilient vegetables that don't fall apart when cooked. These hearty leaves have a hint of bitterness, but the sweetness of the oyster sauce is a nice contrast. This is a beautiful and different side dish to serve at an introductory Vietnamese dinner.

1$^1/_2$ tablespoons oil

6 cloves garlic, chopped

$^1/_4$ cup oyster sauce

2 tablespoons fish sauce

1 teaspoon ground black pepper

4 cups mustard greens,
   approximately $^1/_2$ bunch

2 tablespoons sesame seeds

1. In a large skillet, heat the oil over medium heat. Add the chopped garlic and sauté for 5 minutes.

2. Mix together the oyster sauce, fish sauce, and pepper.

3. Add the mustard greens to the skillet with the oyster sauce mixture and cook for about 5 minutes or until the greens have wilted.

4. Mix in the sesame seeds and serve hot with steamed rice.

[SERVES 2]

SAUTEED TOFU WITH OYSTER SAUCE
Đậu Hủ Xào Dầu Hao

Sautéing tofu is incredibly easy. A number of ingredients can be sautéed with tofu to make for an elaborate dish. However, I appreciate just this simple tofu stir-fry with nothing else but delicious oyster sauce.

1$\frac{1}{2}$ tablespoons oil

4 cups $\frac{3}{4}$-inch-cubed tofu

$\frac{1}{4}$ cup oyster sauce

1 teaspoon ground black pepper

1 tablespoon sugar

3 tablespoons fish sauce

1. In a medium skillet, heat the oil.
2. Add the tofu and remaining ingredients one after the other. Toss the tofu gently as the liquid reduces. Cook over medium heat for about 5 to 8 minutes or until the tofu is tender. Serve immediately with its sauce and steamed rice.

[SERVES 4]

Spiritual life is an important aspect of Little Saigon, and the way the residents conduct business, interact with one another, and struggle with life in this new country is very much anchored to the church and temple life. Catholicism is another very important religion for the Vietnamese. Introduction to Catholicism occurred with the French colonization in the 1850s. The French and their Christian religion represented Western thoughts and ideas, and many Vietnamese initially converted to Catholicism to demonstrate their faith and loyalty to France. But Catholicism has grown beyond that, and today it is the second-largest religion of the Vietnamese.

THE VIETNAMESE WEDDING

When two people fall in love and are ready to be married in a Vietnamese wedding, the wedding date must first be chosen based on the lunar calendar. If they choose an unlucky date, their marriage is doomed.

The wedding day, which is always a Saturday, starts with a knock on the door of the bride's family. The groom and his entourage—his wedding party and the most important of his family members—arrive in a procession with edible gifts as an offering to the bride's family. Placed in tins, the traditional trays of food called trau cau include rice cakes (sticky rice with coconut and mung beans), tea and rice wine, and a whole roasted pig. The bride wears the traditional Vietnamese dress, the ao dai, but for her wedding it is much more elegant and usually red. The groom also wears traditional Vietnamese attire, the male version of the ao dai. At the bride's house, the groom and his family ask for the hand of the bride, and when both parties agree, they pray at the altar and ask for the blessings of their ancestors. Then the bride and her family are invited to the home of the groom's parents, because traditionally, in the past, a woman would move into her husband's family home. At the groom's house, a light lunch is provided for both families and close friends. Then it's off to the church or temple for the religious ceremony.

After the ceremony, there's a very festive reception at one of the high-end seafood restaurants of Little Saigon. The reception (usually with 300 to 500 guests) cannot start until the most respected elders have arrived. As with any wedding, there is a good deal of eating (including a wedding cake), drinking, dancing, and picture taking. It never fails that at the center of the table rests a bucket of ice, a bottle of midpriced cognac, and a two-liter bottle of Sprite or some kind of cola. The Vietnamese love their cognac, another French import. It's the only alcohol I've ever seen consumed or gifted within our culture.

During the evening the wedding couple, along with their parents, stop at each table, exchange blessings, and collect gifts from their guests—envelopes with a generous amount of cash. The Vietnamese do not have any concept of a wedding gift registry; cash has always been the traditional gift. The money traditionally helps the couple to purchase their first car or make a down payment on a home. But these days, it's often used just to pay for the wedding!

Outdoor wedding luncheon in Saigon, 1959. (This is the informal luncheon before the big wedding reception later in the evening.) My grandma is in the middle with my mother to the left in pigtails.

VIETNAMESE WATER SPINACH SAUTEED WITH GARLIC
Rau Mưổng Xào Tỏi

Vietnamese water spinach is prized for its salty but slight bitter flavor. It melds well with garlic and fish sauce. If you can't find it in your market, ask if it can be specially ordered. You can substitute spinach or mustard greens; however, this recipe is about the opportunity to sample this exotic green. Add tofu or additional veggies to the recipe if you wish.

6 cups fresh water spinach

2 tablespoons fish sauce

¼ cup oil

1½ teaspoons sugar

1 shallot, finely chopped

5 cloves garlic, finely chopped

1 tablespoon sesame seeds

1 scallion, chopped into rings

1. Rinse the water spinach and pat it dry. Remove and discard the stems.

2. In a small bowl, stir together the fish sauce, 2 tablespoons of the oil, and the sugar. Set aside.

3. In a medium skillet, warm the remaining oil over medium heat. Add the chopped shallot and garlic and sauté for a few minutes.

4. Add the water spinach leaves to the skillet all at once. Toss the greens while they cook for about 3 to 5 minutes. The leaves will shrink as they are cooking.

5. Next, add the fish sauce mixture to the skillet, pouring it all over the water spinach. Continue tossing for about 3 to 5 minutes so that the spinach is evenly covered with the marinade and the leaves have cooked through or are completely limp. Stir in the sesame seeds and toss to evenly disperse them.

6. Serve hot, garnished with the chopped scallion.

[SERVES 4]

BRAISED EGGPLANT AND TOFU IN CARAMEL SAUCE
Cà Tím Đậu Hủ Kho

Eggplant is one of those vegetables that practically "melt" after a long cooking process, which is why it is so often found in slow-cooked Vietnamese dishes like a curry or a stew. For this dish, the cooking time must be close to an hour in order to achieve the velvety texture of an overcooked eggplant. This is not the most attractive-looking dish, however, so be sure to chop plenty of Thai basil to garnish it.

2 large Asian eggplants (or 2 globe eggplants)

3 tablespoons salt

6 ounces (1 package) firm tofu

3 tablespoons sugar

1 large yellow onion, peeled, quartered, and separated

4 cloves garlic, minced

2 anise seed pods

1/4 cup fish sauce

1/2 fresh Thai bird chile, finely chopped

3/4 cup Coco Rico coconut soda

1 teaspoon ground black pepper

Fresh Thai basil leaves, roughly chopped

1. Wash, pat dry, and peel the eggplants. Cut them into 1 1/2-inch cubes. Place the cubes in a colander or on a baking sheet and generously sprinkle them with the 3 tablespoons of salt to sweat out the bitter juices. Let stand for about 20 minutes. If you are using globe eggplants, increase the salting time to 35 minutes.

2. Rinse the salt off the eggplant cubes and pat them dry. Place the cubes in a medium bowl. Set aside.

3. Cut the tofu into cubes about 2 inches thick.

4. In a clay pot or saucepan, carmelize the sugar. Then, add the eggplant and coat. Add the onion, garlic, anise pods, and a pinch of salt to the eggplant.

5. Add the tofu, fish sauce, chile, coconut soda, and black pepper to the pot. Blend all together and bring to a boil. Lower the heat to a simmer, cover the pot, and let cook for 1 hour, or until the liquid has reduced to a thick sauce.

6. Garnish with the Thai basil and serve with steamed rice.

[SERVES 4]

CABBAGE SALAD WITH BANANA BLOSSOMS
Gỏi Chay Rau Răm Bắp Chuối

This vegetarian salad is distinctive because of the banana blossoms, the flower of the banana plant. Banana blossoms, which have a high content of tannic acid, are popular in soups and salads because of their sour and tangy taste. Here they complement the crunch of the cabbage and the fish sauce. You can also add more ingredients such as tofu or shredded chicken.

1 cup banana blossoms

2 cups water

Juice of 1 lime

1 head green cabbage

½ yellow onion

¼ cup fish sauce

½ teaspoon chili paste

2 tablespoons fresh lime juice

½ tablespoon sugar

¼ cup chopped fresh Thai basil
leaves

¼ cup chopped fresh Vietnamese
coriander leaves

¼ cup chopped fresh mint leaves

½ cup fresh mung bean sprouts

1 tablespoon oil

2 tablespoons sliced shallots

⅓ cup crushed unsalted dry-
roasted peanuts

1. Remove and discard the outer layers of the banana blossoms. Soak the core of the blossoms in a bowl with 2 cups of water and the juice of 1 lime for 20 minutes.

2. While the banana blossoms are soaking, rinse the head of cabbage, then remove the outer layers. Cut the head in half and remove the core. Shred the cabbage with the mandoline, or chop it into small shreds. Put the cabbage in a large bowl.

3. Slice the half onion with a mandoline or cut it into paper-thin slices. Add the onion slices to the shredded cabbage.

4. In a small bowl, combine the fish sauce, chili paste, 2 tablespoons lime juice, and sugar. Whisk until the sugar is dissolved. Set aside.

5. Drain the banana blossoms and pat dry. Julienne the blossoms into thin shreds, and add them to the cabbage and onion mix.

6. Add the chopped basil, coriander, mint leaves, and bean sprouts to the salad bowl. Pour the fish sauce dressing all over the salad and toss.

7. In a small skillet or saucepan, heat 1 tablespoon of oil until hot. Add the sliced shallots and fry until golden brown. Drain.

8. Garnish the salad with the crushed peanuts and fried shallots. Let the salad sit for 10 minutes to allow the cabbage to wilt slightly, and then serve.

[SERVES 4 TO 6]

VEGETARIAN SWEET-AND-SOUR SOUP
Canh Chua Chay

This vegetarian alternative to Canh Chua Ca (see the recipe in the Comfort Foods chapter) is great for those who do not like cooking with a fish carcass. It is one of the more playful dishes that the Vietnamese cuisine has to offer. The pineapple juice, combined with the tomatoes and herbs, makes for an extremely fragrant and complex dish. The little bit of heat in the soup hits you perfectly in the back of the throat. Taro stems may be hard to find, but keep looking; you can substitute celery, but only after you have exhausted all resources.

6 cups unsweetened pineapple juice

4 cups water

1 teaspoon ground black pepper

1/2 tablespoon sugar

1 cup 1/4-inch sliced taro stems

6 tablespoons fish sauce

1/2 cup fresh or canned bamboo
   shoots

2 shallots, finely chopped

3 whole cloves garlic

3 tomatoes, each cut into 6 pieces

1 stalk lemongrass, cut into 3-inch
   lengths

1 1/2 fresh Thai bird chiles, finely
   chopped

1 cup diced fresh or canned pineapple

2 scallions, chopped into rings

1 cup fresh mung bean sprouts

3 cups cooked rice vermicelli
   (optional)

1 cup diced tofu (optional)

Fresh cilantro

1. In a large stockpot, combine the pineapple juice and water and bring to a rolling boil. Add the black pepper, sugar, taro stems, fish sauce, bamboo shoots, shallots, garlic, tomatoes, lemongrass, and chopped chiles to the boiling broth. Lower the heat and let the soup simmer for 20 minutes. Add the diced pineapple and scallions and continue cooking for another 5 minutes.

2. When ready to serve, stir in the bean sprouts and, if desired, the cooked noodles or tofu. Garnish with the fresh cilantro.

[SERVES 6]

When families have lost a loved one, they will give a picture of the deceased to a temple, where it is displayed on a wall among hundreds of other photographs; this can be quite an overwhelming sight for the visitor. The monks, wearing their gold or saffron robes, will sit with other temple members to pray for these souls, so that they reach Nirvana.

Seafood Dishes

THE FISH MARKETS

You need to take only a quick look at a map of Vietnam to see why seafood stands out in our cuisine. With the country's long coastline and extensive Mekong River system, it's obvious why seafood is predominantly showcased at the Vietnamese table—both in Vietnam itself as well as in Little Saigon. Not only is seafood served with every lunch or dinner meal, but it is even served at breakfast (such as our rice porridge with braised catfish or shrimp).

Little Saigon's individual fish markets as well as the large seafood sections of the Vietnamese markets offer an ocean bounty that far surpasses any American market. They are the sole source of fresh (and inexpensive) seafood for the community. The Vietnamese fishmongers in Little Saigon are true professionals in their field. Provided there is no language barrier, the fishmonger can offer information about the flavor, freshness, and quality of every type of fish and will steer the customer in the right direction to create the perfect seafood dish. The community is so small and close-knit, any fishmonger or market selling poor quality seafood would quickly go out of business.

The layout from one store to the next is consistent. Refrigerated glass cases within every market are stocked with fish fillets and steaks. Below these cases are trays holding an oceanful of whole fish on ice for consumers to pick up and prod—snapper, sea bass, mackerel, and geoduck, just to name a few. The fish come without markers, but the locals are always able to identify what they need. White plastic buckets hold various mollusks like clams or mussels, still alive and gurgling in salt water. Above it all are several gigantic tanks with schools of fish like tilapia, catfish, and Dover sole, which can be purchased straight from the tank. Another tank is for Dungeness crab, and a third for lobster; customers reach in to take a crab or lobster right out of the tank to check the size and health of the creature.

Because the freshness of the seafood is of the highest importance in Vietnamese cuisine, the majority of our fish dishes are prepared simply—steamed, boiled, or pan-fried with little fanfare other than a little bit of fresh lemongrass or ginger to liven them up. The notion of melted butter or elaborate, thick sauces for seafood is inconceivable. Shellfish, cooked by simple boiling or steaming, are enjoyed with just some herbs, and a lime, salt, and pepper mixture for dipping. Instead of fish steaks and fillets, a whole fish is often steamed or grilled and served with its head, tail, skin, and bones intact. The Vietnamese believe that when a fish is cooked whole, it has more juiciness and flavor. Similarly, shrimp are cooked with their tails and shells on to retain their taste and essence.

The recipes in this chapter include simple ones as well as a few more involved ones such as stir-fries or curries. Some you will fall in love with and want to try again and again with every different type of fish. Just remember, to cook as the Vietnamese do, you want to start with the freshest possible seafood.

The Vietnamese believe it is best to cook a whole fish with the bones and skin intact. It may seem bothersome to pick out fish bones from your mouth as you're eating, but it's worth it for the flavor. If you feel you must debone the cooked fish before serving, lift the flesh gently to remove the bones, then skewer the fish back together for presentation's sake. It just takes practice.

WHOLE SALTED FISH WITH LEMONGRASS AND CHILI PASTE
Cá Chiên Xã Ốt

Even though the Vietnamese enjoy grilling their seafood, we really love frying as well. A perfectly fried whole fish has phenomenal flavor and an addictive crunch. The crispy, fried fish skin is half the fun, but it also absorbs most of the salty fish sauce. The lime cuts through the saltiness, as does the steamed rice. If you would like to try this recipe with skinless fish fillets, cut the amount of fish sauce in half. This dish is popular at home as well as on the lazy Susan for a large group of people at a celebratory meal.

3/4 pound whole mackerel or
    tilapia, with skin

6 cloves garlic

3 stalks fresh lemongrass, finely
    chopped

1/4 onion, finely chopped

1/2 tablespoon sugar

1/4 cup fish sauce

1 teaspoon chili paste

1/3 cup oil for frying

1 scallion, chopped into rings

1 lime, halved

1. Clean the fish thoroughly and remove the entrails if your fishmonger has not already done so. On each side of the fish, cut three diagonal, evenly spaced slashes, cutting almost to the bone. Pat dry.

2. In a mortar with a pestle, pound together the garlic, lemongrass, onion, and sugar. Put the ingredients in a small bowl. Add the fish sauce and chili paste and whisk together with a fork.

3. Spread the paste over the fish, making sure to rub between the slashes as well. Set the fish aside and let it marinate for an hour.

4. In a skillet large enough to fit the whole fish, heat the oil over high heat for about 5 minutes. Carefully place the fish in the skillet and fry for about 5 to 8 minutes or until the skin is golden brown and crispy. The length of time will depend on the thickness of your fish. Check for doneness by slightly lifting the fish and looking on its underside, and check between the slashes to see that the fish is cooked through. The fish will be white and flaky.

5. Flip the fish over and fry for another 5 minutes, until golden brown, over high heat. Garnish the fish with the scallions, and squeeze half the lime over the entire fish. Reserve half the lime for guests who would like more. Serve fish with a lot of steamed rice.

[SERVES 4]

GRILLED SALTED FISH WITH LIME
Cá Muối Nướng

The Vietnamese love their salted dishes, and salty seafood is no exception. In many recipes, seasonings like salt are often taken for granted. We do not have that situation here. We use an appetizing salt rub that permeates the skin of the fish and makes it nice and crispy. Mackerel has a high oil content, which makes it a perfect candidate for grilling. If you prefer another fish, ask your fishmonger for the freshest oily white fish available. For this recipe, and for grilled fish in general, you really need to use a whole fish, preferably not deboned, as fillets tend to flake and fall apart while grilling. If you feel you must debone your whole fish before cooking it, stuff it with scallions and tie it up with cooking twine so that it maintains its shape. The skin needs to stay on, as this is what keeps the flesh intact while grilling.

1 pound whole mackerel or another
   oily white fish, with skin

¼ cup coarse salt

1 teaspoon chili paste

8 cloves garlic, minced

¼ cup finely chopped onion

½ tablespoon sugar

3 tablespoons oil for brushing

Juice of ½ medium lime

1 scallion, chopped into rings

1. Clean the fish thoroughly and remove the entrails if your fishmonger has not already done so. On each side of the fish, cut three evenly spaced, diagonal slashes, cutting almost to the bone. These slashes are important because they will help the seasonings penetrate the flesh. Pat dry.

2. In a small bowl, combine the coarse salt, chili paste, minced garlic, chopped onion, and sugar. Blend well so that it forms a paste.

3. Spread the paste all over the fish, making sure to rub between the slashes as well. Cover the fish, refrigerate, and let it marinate for at least 8 hours. For best results, the fish should marinate overnight.

4. Before grilling, lightly rinse the salt off the fish, but the salt inside the slashes of the fish can remain. The salt paste does not need to be completely rinsed off.

5. Over medium heat, heat a grill large enough to fit the whole fish. Brush the fish all over with the oil. If the fish has been deboned, stuff it with scallions and tie it together with cooking twine.

6. Place the fish on the hot grill and cook for about 5 minutes on each side or until the skin is blackened and crispy. Lift the fish gently to check the underside for color and crispness. Look inside the slashes

to check that the fish is cooked; the flesh should be white and tender and slightly flaky. Remove the fish from the grill and lay it on a large platter.

7. Squeeze the juice of half a lime all over the entire fish. Garnish with the chopped scallions and serve over bun or with lots of steamed rice.

[SERVES 4]

FRIED FISH FILLETS WITH LEMONGRASS
Cá Chiên Xã

The clean and light flavors of this recipe require that you select a meaty fish such as mackerel, catfish, or sea bass, because certain types of fish won't stand up to the hot frying oil. This is a great, palatable dish that's very common in Vietnamese cuisine, but it is *salty!* It originated as a way to make a small amount of food stretch for many as an entire meal. The fish fillets turn a nice golden brown when fried, and the addition of lemongrass gives them a fragrant, lemony taste to contrast with the salt. Eat this fish with lots of rice or bun and dip tiny bites into tangy nuoc cham.

3/4 to 1 pound fish fillets or steaks

1/2 teaspoon salt

1/2 tablespoon sugar

1 teaspoon chili paste

1 tablespoon fish sauce

1 tablespoon fresh lime juice

1/2 teaspoon ground black pepper

**2 tablespoons finely chopped
  fresh lemongrass**

2 tablespoons oil

5 cloves garlic, finely chopped

1. Clean the fish fillets or steaks and pat dry. Place them in a shallow dish.

2. Combine the salt and sugar in a bowl. Sprinkle the mixture evenly all over both sides of the fish. Cover and let sit for at least 8 hours in the refrigerator; overnight is ideal.

3. Remove the fish from the refrigerator. The salt and sugar should have penetrated the fish, and there should be liquid in the dish, as the salt extracts water from the fish. Drain off any water from the dish.

4. In a small bowl, whisk together the chili paste, fish sauce, lime juice, black pepper, and lemongrass.

5. In a large skillet, heat the oil over medium heat. Begin by frying the chopped garlic for a few minutes or until golden brown. Then add the fish fillets or steaks. Drizzle the fish sauce mixture all over the fish and fry for 5 minutes per side.

6. Serve the fish hot with bun or with plenty of steamed rice, nuoc cham, and the salad platter.

[SERVES 4]

Cá Hấp Gừng Hành

Steaming a whole fish is a way to appreciate a perfect, fresh, and beautiful fish; you are not hiding anything by covering it with a glaze or by pan-frying it in a sauce. For this recipe, the fish can be prepared without the bones, but the cavity needs to be filled with herbs and skewered closed so that the shape is maintained. This recipe is an ideal way to cook a variety of fish; I have enjoyed it with halibut, king mackerel, and sea bass.

3 tablespoons soy sauce

1/4 cup fish sauce

1 fresh Thai bird chile, finely chopped

1 medium-size piece fresh ginger (approximately 1/4 size of a palm), peeled and cut into thin slivers 1 1/2 to 2 inches in length

1 1/2 tablespoons ground black pepper

1 1/2 tablespoons sugar

7 tablespoons oil

1/2 tablespoon fresh lime juice

1 pound whole tilapia or other flat fish with firm white flesh

5 scallions

1/2 large yellow onion, cut into thin slices

Fresh cilantro

1. To begin, you will need to prepare two marinades, one that the fish will be steamed in and another that will be drizzled over the cooked fish. To make the first marinade, combine in a small bowl 2 tablespoons soy sauce, 3 tablespoons fish sauce, chopped chile, ginger slices, 1 tablespoon black pepper, 1 tablespoon sugar, and 1/4 cup oil. Whisk until the sugar is dissolved and the olive oil has emulsified with the soy sauce. Set aside.

2. For the second marinade, whisk together in a separate bowl 1 tablespoon soy sauce, 1 tablespoon fish sauce, 1/2 tablespoon black pepper, 1/2 tablespoon sugar, 3 tablespoons oil, and 1/2 tablespoon lime juice. Whisk until the sugar is dissolved and the oil, soy sauce, and lime juice have emulsified. Set aside.

3. Begin by cleaning the fish, removing the entrails but leaving the bones and skin intact, if the fishmonger has not already done so for you. On each side of the fish, cut three diagonal slashes, evenly spaced and cutting almost halfway to the bone (or cavity if you have deboned the fish).

4. Cut 3 of the scallions into 4-inch pieces. Stuff the scallions and half of the onion slices into the cavity of the fish. Cut the remaining scallions into 2-inch pieces and, with the remaining sliced onions, create a bed for the fish in a shallow, heat-resistant china dish or pie pan.

5. Place the fish in the dish or pie pan over the bed of scallions and onions. Pour the marinade for the steamed fish (it's the marinade that is larger in quantity) all over the fish, coating it entirely and making sure that the liquid penetrates the flesh through the slashes. Cover and refrigerate for 25 minutes.

6. Prepare the steamer. When the water begins to boil, uncover the fish and place the dish in the steamer. Steam for about 5 to 8 minutes. Check for doneness every few minutes by studying the slits of the fish. The fish should be flaky but firm to the touch, and the flesh should be whitened.

7. Remove the dish from the steamer and immediately drizzle the second marinade over the entire fish. Garnish with the cilantro and serve immediately with steamed rice and the salad platter.

[SERVES 4]

When purchasing a fresh whole fish, clear eyes are not always a sign of freshness. Observe the flesh of the fish, looking for a translucent, not dry or flaky, quality. When in doubt, always ask your friend the fishmonger. If you're looking for fish steaks or fillets, choose the belly cut, which is mostly marbled in fat. With steaks and fillets it is hard to tell if the fish is fresh, which is why we like to have whole fish, because you can see the freshness in the skin and sometimes the eyes.

HANOI-STYLE FRIED FISH WITH TURMERIC AND DILL
Chả Cá Thăng Long

Over a hundred years ago, this dish was introduced for the first time in a restaurant at 14 Cha Ca Street in Hanoi, in an area now known as the Old Quarter. The appeal of cha ca came from its great taste, but also from its elaborate presentation. Clearly intended for those who want to enjoy a long meal, the dish is served with numerous bowls of condiments and sauces. This recipe incorporates dill and turmeric, which are more common in northern Vietnam than in any other region of the country. Another version of this Hanoi dish has the monkfish skewered with thin sugarcane sticks and grilled.

1¹/₂ pounds whole monkfish or other hearty white fish like mackerel, with skin intact, or skinless monkfish or mackerel fillets

¹/₂ teaspoon salt

3 tablespoons fish sauce

1 tablespoon minced fresh ginger

2 scallions, chopped into rings

1 tablespoon sugar

1 teaspoon ground black pepper

1 tablespoon ground turmeric

1¹/₂ cups rice flour

2 bunches of fresh dill, chopped

¹/₂ cup sesame seed or peanut oil

2 cups cooked rice vermicelli (bun)

¹/₂ large onion, sliced into rings

¹/₂ cup chopped fresh cilantro leaves

INDIVIDUAL BOWLS TO BE SERVED WITH FISH:

¹/₂ cup unsalted dry-roasted peanuts

¹/₃ cup dipping sauce

¹/₄ cup soy sauce

¹/₃ cup chopped fresh dill

Picked shallots

Pickled carrots

1 lime, quartered

1. Clean the whole fish thoroughly and remove the entrails if your fishmonger has not already done so. On each side of the fish, cut three diagonal, evenly spaced slashes, cutting halfway to the bone. The slashes will allow the herbs and spices to reach the flesh of the fish. Pat fish completely dry and place in a shallow dish.

2. Lightly coat the fish all over with the salt. Cover and refrigerate for at least an hour. (If you decide to cook with fish fillets, cut them into 2-inch cubes and marinate for only 15 minutes.)

3. In a small bowl, combine the fish sauce, ginger, scallions, sugar, and pepper. Whisk until the sugar is dissolved. Remove the fish from the refrigerator, and rub it all over with the sauce to completely cover it.

4. Sprinkle the turmeric all over the fish, about $\frac{1}{2}$ tablespoon on each side. Cover and refrigerate for another 20 minutes.

5. Fill a shallow dish or large bowl with the rice flour. Take the fish from the marinade and place it in the rice flour to very lightly coat it. If it is easier, you can also lightly sprinkle the rice flour over the fish with your hands and dust off any excess flour.

6. If you are using a whole fish, stuff the inside of the fish with half of the dill. The dill does not need to be entirely inside the fish; much of it can be exposed. For grilling fish pieces, roughly chop one bunch of the fresh dill and toss over the pieces.

7. Meanwhile, in a skillet large enough to fit the fish, heat the oil over high heat. When hot, gently place the fish in the oil. Fry the fish over high heat until it is crispy and golden brown, about 8 minutes on each side. For fish cubes, cook for about 5 to 8 minutes, tossing the fish until evenly cooked and golden brown.

8. While the fish is frying, prepare a bed of the cooked rice vermicelli and remaining dill on a serving platter. Place the cooked fish directly on top.

9. In the hot oil, fry the onions for about 3 minutes. Place them on top of the fish and garnish with the cilantro.

10. Serve the fish hot, with steamed rice, salad platter, and the individual bowls of condiments and sauces. Each person will take large pieces of fish and noodles at one time, then wrap that morsel with herbs and lettuce from the salad platter, and finally dip each bite into nuoc cham.

[SERVES 4]

SALT AND PEPPER FRIED SHRIMP
Tom Rang Muối

Vietnamese wedding receptions are often like seafood banquets. One dish that is a must to serve is this succulent salted and peppered shrimp. Still in its shell and with its head intact, the shrimp is pan-fried with black pepper, salt, and garlic in a nice butter bath. Butter is rarely used in Vietnamese food, which is why this is such a decadent dish. The shell is softened to an edible chew, so try eating the whole shrimp with its shell as the Vietnamese do. You will be utterly surprised how flavorful and addictive these shrimp can be. The rice flour and cornstarch give a perfect crunch, and the texture is extraordinary.

1 pound fresh medium shrimp,
    with or without heads, but shells
    and tails intact
2^1/2 tablespoons salt
4 cups warm water
3 tablespoons rice flour
3 tablespoons cornstarch
1^1/2 teaspoons ground black
    pepper
^{1}/2 teaspoon sugar
4 cloves garlic, finely chopped
2 tablespoons oil
3 tablespoons butter
2 shallots, diced
2 scallions, chopped into rings
1 fresh red Thai bird chile,
    chopped into rings

1. Clean the shrimp thoroughly. In a medium bowl, dissolve 2 tablespoons of the salt in the 4 cups of water. Soak the shrimp in the salt water for an hour. Then drain and pat dry.

2. In a small bowl, combine the rice flour, cornstarch, pepper, sugar, garlic, and remaining ^{1}/2 tablespoon of salt. Stir until thoroughly blended.

3. Pour the dry ingredients from the bowl into a plastic or ziplock bag. It should be a large enough bag to fit all the shrimp. Place all the shrimp in the bag and shake so that the flour mixture lightly coats the shrimp. If you'd prefer, you can mix the shrimp with the dry ingredients in a large mixing bowl.

4. Heat the oil and 2 tablespoons of butter in a wok or large saucepan over high heat. When hot, throw in the shallots, stirring quickly for 5 minutes. Then reduce the heat to medium and add the remaining tablespoon of butter and the red chile.

5. Toss in the flour-coated shrimp and stir quickly for 5 minutes or until they are pink and the flour has browned.

6. Add the scallions, garnish with more black pepper, and serve hot in a large bowl or platter.

[SERVES 4]

GRILLED SHRIMP WITH GARLIC, LEMONGRASS, AND CHILI PASTE
Tom Nướng Tỏi Xã Ốt

Like most other seafoods, when shrimp is grilled on a grill pan or barbecue, it takes on a strong, smoky scent. The smoke brings out the garlic and lemongrass. But alternatively, you can pan-fry or sauté the shrimp in the marinade to create a sauce to drizzle over your steamed rice or noodles— preferably an herb noodle salad. Just a little bit of fresh mint is all the accent you need.

1 tablespoon finely chopped fresh lemongrass

5 cloves garlic, minced

¼ teaspoon chili paste

3 tablespoons fish sauce

1 teaspoon sugar

2 tablespoons oil

1 tablespoon fresh lime juice

½ tablespoon black pepper

2 tablespoons finely chopped scallions

½ pound fresh medium shrimp, peeled, deveined, tails intact

1 medium onion, cut into 6 pieces and separated

Chopped fresh mint

1. In a medium bowl, whisk together the lemongrass, garlic, chili paste, fish sauce, sugar, oil, lime juice, pepper, and scallions until the sugar is dissolved.

2. Add the shrimp to the bowl and toss so that all the shrimp are completely coated with the marinade. Cover the bowl and let it sit for about 15 minutes in the refrigerator.

3. Prepare the grill. While it is heating, skewer the shrimp and onion, alternating between them. Lightly brush with marinade.

4. Place the skewers over the hot grill. Brush again with any remaining marinade. Cook for about 8 to 10 minutes, turning the shrimp over just once. The shrimp are cooked when they have turned pinkish in color and curled slightly.

5. Garnish the shrimp and onion skewers with the chopped mint and serve with nuoc cham as an appetizer. Or serve with rice or bun for a meal.

[SERVES 2 AS AN ENTREE OR 4 AS AN APPETIZER]

FRIED SHRIMP WITH SHRIMP PASTE, LEMONGRASS, AND CHILI PASTE
Tom Xào Mắm Ruoc Tỏi Ớt

Fermented shrimp paste has long been popular to flavor soups and braise meats. We take fresh shrimp, add some shrimp paste, and get some of the best umami-tasting dishes. It's like taking a bite out of the ocean. The briny taste of shrimp, coupled with the lemongrass and light touch of chili paste is something I crave at times. This perfectly balanced dish is accomplished by lightly frying the shrimp; only then are all the ingredients' flavors completely revealed.

1 tablespoon finely chopped fresh
    lemongrass
1/2 teaspoon chili paste
2 tablespoons fish sauce
1/2 tablespoon ground black
    pepper
1/2 tablespoon sugar
1/2 tablespoon fresh lime juice
1 tablespoon finely chopped
    scallions
1/2 pound fresh medium shrimp,
    peeled, deveined, tails intact
1/4 cup oil
4 cloves garlic, roughly chopped
11/2 tablespoons shrimp paste
Chopped fresh Chinese parsley
    or plain parsley

1. In a medium bowl, whisk together the lemongrass, chili paste, fish sauce, black pepper, sugar, lime juice, and scallions until the sugar is dissolved.

2. Add the shrimp to the bowl and toss so the marinade completely coats the shrimp. Cover and refrigerate for at least a half hour.

3. In a large skillet, heat the oil over high heat. When the oil is hot, fry the garlic for about 3 minutes until it is fragrant and golden to dark brown.

4. Remove the shrimp from the marinade; reserve the marinade. Fry the shrimp in the hot oil with the garlic. Cook for about 5 minutes, over high heat, turning the shrimp once. When the shrimp are done, they will have curled and turned pink in color.

5. Discard half of the oil from the skillet and lower the heat to medium.

6. Whisk the shrimp paste into the remaining marinade, and add the mixture to the shrimp in the skillet. Blend the marinade, the shrimp, and the oil, and serve immediately, garnished with parsley. Serve with generous amounts of steamed rice.

[SERVES 4]

FRIED SHRIMP IN TURMERIC AND GARLIC BATTER
Tom Chiên Lang Bột

Vietnamese cuisine does not have a real appetizer course, since the meal is generally served all at once, family-style. When I am in the mood for something a little bit different and would like to make a statement to open a meal, I turn to this simple dish of fried shrimp with garlic and turmeric. It can be served as a simple side dish as well. The turmeric gives the shrimp an almost unnatural bright yellow color, which is quite pleasing and interesting to the eye. The light coating of rice flour gives the shrimp a perfect, light crispiness. You can hardly even call it a batter, which makes it all the more appealing in texture. The shrimp is made even better once it is dipped into nuoc cham or, for a more Western taste, mayonnaise.

1 cup rice flour

1 cup cornstarch

1 1/2 tablespoons ground turmeric

1 medium head garlic, about
   10 cloves, separated, peeled,
   and finely chopped

1 tablespoon ground black pepper

3 tablespoons salt

1/2 teaspoon sugar

1 1/2 cups sesame seed oil

1 pound fresh large shrimp,
   peeled, deveined, tails intact

1/4 lime

1. In a medium bowl, combine the rice flour, cornstarch, turmeric, garlic, pepper, salt, and sugar. Stir until evenly mixed.

2. In a skillet, heat the sesame seed oil over high heat until it reaches 340 degrees.

3. While the oil is heating, lightly coat the shrimp, one at a time, all over with the rice flour mixture. The shrimp should then be placed directly into the hot oil. Alternatively, you can place the flour mixture in a plastic bag, add all of the shrimp, and shake the bag to give the shrimp an even, light coating. Make sure you work quickly as you dredge the shrimp in flour and then fry them in the hot oil, as the cornstarch tends to clump if you coat the shrimp too early.

4. Fry the shrimp a few at a time, over high heat, for about 2 minutes on each side, turning the shrimp just once. When done, the shrimp should be golden brown and yellow from the turmeric, and firm to the touch. Transfer the shrimp to drain on paper towels.

5. Squeeze lime over the fried shrimp before serving. Serve hot with nuoc cham.

[SERVES 4 AS AN APPETIZER]

SNOW PEAS AND SHRIMP SAUTEED IN GARLIC AND OYSTER SAUCE

Đậu Xào Tom

This popular Chinese-style dish is served at most large restaurant banquets or as a simple side dish at home. It is a great entree that combines different flavors: the sweetness of the snow peas, the umami of the shrimp, and the saltiness of the oyster sauce. Substituting tofu for the shrimp turns this into a great vegetarian dish. Long green beans can be substituted if snow peas are not available.

1 cup fresh snow peas

3 tablespoons fish sauce

3 tablespoons oyster sauce

1 fresh Thai bird chile, finely chopped

1 teaspoon ground black pepper

$1/2$ teaspoon sugar

$2/3$ pound fresh small or medium shrimp, peeled, deveined, tails intact

2 tablespoons oil

1 large onion, cut into 6 parts and separated

5 cloves garlic, finely chopped

1 medium carrot, cut into $1/4$-inch slices

$1/2$ cup fresh or canned straw mushrooms

$1/4$ cup cashews

Fresh cilantro

1. Bring a pot of water to a rolling boil and blanch the snow peas for 2 minutes. Remove them from the boiling water and immediately place them in a bowl of ice water.

2. In a small bowl, combine the fish sauce, oyster sauce, chopped chile, black pepper, and sugar. Whisk until the sugar is dissolved. Add the raw shrimp to the bowl and set aside to marinate for 15 minutes.

3. In a large skillet, heat the oil over medium heat. Sauté the onions for 5 minutes before adding the garlic and cooking for another 3 minutes.

4. With the skillet still on medium heat, add the sliced carrots and cook for several minutes, stirring quickly so that they cook evenly. Stir in the mushrooms and continue cooking and stirring for a few more minutes.

5. Then add the shrimp and marinade and cook for another 5 minutes. Follow immediately with the snow peas. Cook for another few minutes, just until the peas and shrimp are warm.

6. Remove the pan from the heat, stir in the cashews, and garnish with the cilantro. Serve with steamed rice.

[SERVES 4]

SPICY SHRIMP WITH TOFU AND EGGPLANT IN
COCONUT AND GINGER YELLOW CURRY
Cà-rí Tom Đậu Hủ

Not for the faint of heart, this spicy curry dish requires that you slowly cook its ingredients in a clay pot or saucepan. Take a heaping spoonful of this curry with the shrimp, tofu, and eggplant, and pour it over your bowl of steamed rice or rice vermicelli. Then shred a variety of herbs from the salad platter on top and enjoy. If you are averse to the heat of the dish, decrease the chili paste by half or do not add it all.

1 Japanese or Chinese eggplant,
    peeled and sliced across

4 tablespoons salt

6 ounces (1 package) firm tofu

3 tablespoons fish sauce

2 tablespoons finely chopped
    fresh ginger

2 scallions, chopped into rings

1 teaspoon chili paste

1/2 tablespoon ground turmeric

1/2 pound fresh medium shrimp,
    peeled, deveined, tails intact

2 tablespoons oil

1 yellow onion, cut into 6 pieces

1/2 cup chicken broth or water

1/2 tablespoon cumin

2 tablespoons yellow curry powder

11/2 cups coconut milk

1/2 teaspoon black peppercorns

1. Cut the eggplant into 1-inch cubes and salt them generously; set aside for 20 minutes to sweat out bitterness and impurities.

2. Cut the tofu into cubes, a minimum of 1 inch in size.

3. In a small bowl, combine the fish sauce, ginger, scallions, chili paste, and turmeric. Blend thoroughly and then add the shrimp. Let marinate for 15 minutes.

4. In a clay pot or large saucepan, heat the oil over medium heat. Separate the pieces of the yellow onion and cook for a few minutes. Rinse the eggplant cubes, pat dry, and add them to the pan. Cover and let cook over low heat for 25 minutes or until the eggplant is extremely soft.

5. Add the shrimp and its marinade and the chicken broth or water to the eggplant. Raise the heat to high and bring the mixture to a rolling boil. Boil for 5 minutes, then reduce the heat to a simmer.

6. Slowly stir in the cumin, curry powder, and coconut milk, and cook for 5 to 8 minutes. Add the tofu and peppercorns and continue simmering for another 10 minutes. The curry should be soupy.

7. Serve hot with steamed rice or noodles and a salad platter.

[SERVES 4]

FRIED SQUID IN RICE FLOUR BATTER
Mực Chiên Lang Bột

To be truthful, fried squid is not the most popular dish on a Little Saigon menu, though it's often served at nhau (a night of food and heavy drinking of beer and rice wine). If you are a calamari lover as I am (the American in me can't say no to the tastiness of fried foods), this is an easy dish to make at home. The rice flour coating becomes lightly crispy and is delicious with the sweet tang and saltiness of the dipping sauce.

1 3/4 to 2 pounds fresh squid

1/3 cup fish sauce

1 fresh Thai bird chile, finely chopped

1 cup rice flour

1/2 cup cornstarch

2 tablespoons salt

1 tablespoon ground black pepper

1 tablespoon sugar

1 cup oil

Scallions, chopped into rings

1. Begin by cleaning the squid, separating the head and the body, and removing the pen, head, and membrane. Cut the bodies lengthwise into 1 1/2-inch strips or into rings. Reserve the tentacles for frying as well. Rinse the pieces of squid and pat them dry.

2. Put the squid in a medium bowl. Add the fish sauce and chopped chile. Coat the pieces of squid evenly. Let them soak in the sauce for 15 minutes.

3. In a shallow dish, combine the rice flour, cornstarch, salt, black pepper, and sugar. Stir to completely blend the dry ingredients together.

4. Pour the oil into a medium skillet to a depth of about 1 to 1 1/2 inches. Heat the oil over high heat until it reaches 345 degrees. Line up the dish of squid and fish sauce right next to the dish of dry ingredients.

5. Remove each squid piece from the fish sauce and dredge completely in the flour mixture. Transfer immediately in small batches to the hot oil and deep-fry for 5 minutes, or until the coating has turned golden brown. Drain the fried squid on paper towels.

6. Put the squid in a serving dish and garnish with the chopped scallions. Serve with nuoc cham.

[SERVES 6 AS AN APPETIZER]

MUSSELS SAUTEED WITH CHILES AND THAI BASIL
Nghêu Xào Lá Quê Ốt

When it comes to mussels or clams, we prefer to just steam or boil them before eating them over a newspaper spread on the table. But once in a while, it is a treat to make this Chinese-style dish. The meaty mussels have a nice sweet and salty sauce, with a little bit of a kick from the heat of the chiles. Clams can certainly be substituted for the mussels.

2 pounds fresh mussels

1/4 cup olive or vegetable oil

3 tablespoons finely chopped
   onions

5 cloves garlic, finely chopped

1/2 teaspoon sugar

1 1/2 teaspoons ground black
   pepper

1/4 cup oyster sauce

1 tablespoon fish sauce

2 fresh Thai bird chiles, finely
   chopped

1 tablespoon fresh lime juice

1 1/2 cups chicken broth

1 cup roughly chopped fresh Thai
   basil leaves

1/2 tablespoon cornstarch

2 scallions, chopped into rings

1. Clean and scrub the mussels thoroughly. Discard any with shells that are already open or broken.

2. Heat the oil in a large skillet over medium heat until hot. Sauté the onions and garlic for several minutes until the onions are translucent.

3. In a small bowl, combine the sugar, black pepper, oyster sauce, fish sauce, chopped chiles, and lime juice. Whisk until the sugar is dissolved.

4. Add the mussels to the skillet. Let them cook for 2 minutes, and then drizzle the fish sauce marinade all over them. Stir the mussels with the marinade for a few minutes and then add the chicken broth. Add the chopped basil and toss. Cover the skillet and cook for another 8 minutes.

5. When the mussel shells have opened, add the cornstarch to thicken the liquid, being sure to evenly blend it in. Toss in the scallions.

6. Place the mussels and sauce in a large shallow bowl or on a large serving platter, and serve hot with steamed rice.

[SERVES 4]

FRESH CRAB SAUTEED IN SALT AND PEPPER
Cua Rang Muối

Served at practically every restaurant during a wedding reception or family gathering, cua rang muoi is a popular item simply because it is a fantastic dish that many think is too laborious to make at home. Cua rang muoi should be served as one course among many other courses. This recipe requires that the crab be served with its shell still on but broken, so that the flavors will permeate the meat; that also makes it easier for your diners to eat. The recipe calls for a lot of salt and black pepper, but because you're cooking the crab in the shell, it's not overpowered by the salt or pepper. Cua rang muoi is a hands-on dish and therefore is not served with utensils. If possible, try to get the freshest crab possible rather than a frozen one. There is a popular variation of this dish made with lobster, called tom hum (lobster) rang muoi. Feel free to simply replace the crab in this recipe with lobster.

2 large Dungeness crabs (approximately 2 pounds), freshly cooked

6 tablespoons rice flour

6 tablespoons cornstarch

1 tablespoon sugar

1/4 cup salt

1/4 cup ground black pepper

1/2 cup olive oil

3 large shallots, diced

10 cloves garlic, finely chopped

2 fresh Thai bird chiles, finely chopped

2 tablespoons butter

3 scallions, finely chopped

1. Begin by taking apart the cooked crabs. Remove the claws and legs from the body. Open the body by either cutting the crab in half with a cleaver or pulling the cap from the shell. Discard shell, gills, and so on. The body of the crab should be kept within the cartilage. Rinse the body of the crab. Break the shell of the crab legs and claws with the back of a cleaver or mallet. Place all the crab parts in a shallow dish or on a baking sheet.

2. In a large bowl, combine the flour, cornstarch, sugar, salt, and pepper. Stir until thoroughly blended.

3. Sprinkle the flour mixture all over the crab legs, claws, and body to give them a nice even coating. Use your hands to make sure everything is well coated.

4. Heat the oil in a wok or large saucepan over high heat. When hot, throw in the shallots and stir quickly for 2 minutes. Add the garlic, chiles, and butter over high heat.

5. Toss in the flour-coated crabs and stir quickly for 5 minutes, then add the scallions. Lower the heat to medium and let cook for 10 minutes. The crabs will be a golden brown from the flour mixture.

6. Garnish with more black pepper and serve hot.

[SERVES 4]

DRUNKEN CRAB
Cua Nấu Bia

Here's an easy and imaginative approach to boiling crab. Ideally, when it comes to cooking any shellfish with beer, you should use flat beer, because fresh beer tends to give the shellfish a metallic taste. Do not bother washing the crabs, as this will make them lose their briny taste. Spread some newspapers over the table and enjoy eating the crabs with a blend of salt, pepper, and lime. Salt and pepper are for flavoring, and the acidity of the lime helps to cut the crabs' richness. Hint: I think it makes for a more comprehensive and holistic cooking experience if you are drinking some of the beer involved in preparing this dish. I encourage drinking a cold one as an excellent counterpoint to boiling the crab in the boiling beer. I discourage drinking a cold one while driving home after purchasing your fresh crab.

3 12-ounce cans beer

2 tablespoons oyster sauce

1/4 cup fish sauce

2 tablespoons ground black
   pepper

1 yellow onion, quartered

3 shallots, halved

1 tablespoon coarse salt

6 whole cloves garlic, peeled

3 limes, halved

6 cups water (more or less to
   cover crabs with liquid)

2 live large Dungeness crabs,
   approximately 2 pounds

1. Pour the beer into a large stockpot. Put the pot on medium heat. Add the oyster sauce, fish sauce, 1 1/2 tablespoons of the black pepper, the onion, shallots, 1/2 tablespoon of the salt, the garlic cloves, and 4 of the lime halves to the pot. Stir until the salt and oyster sauce are dissolved.

2. Bring the liquid to a boil. Just as it begins to boil, add the live crabs. Add additional water if needed to completely cover them. Cover the pot and cook over medium heat. The crabs will be cooked after about 15 minutes, or when their shells have turned pinkish orange.

3. Remove the crabs from the pot and let them cool a little.

4. Prepare a salt and pepper dip by combining the remaining 1/2 tablespoon of salt and 1/2 tablespoon of black pepper and the juice of 1 lime. Stir until well mixed.

5. Split the crabs in half. Serve your guests with half a crab each, and give them the proper crab utensils. Place the salt and pepper dip alongside the crabs.

[SERVES 4]

Vietnamese Celebrations and Feasts

THE LAZY SUSAN

If you are in Little Saigon on any given Friday or Saturday evening, peek into one of the banquet-style restaurants and you are sure to notice lively groups crowded around big round tables in a great big dining room. Waiters hurry back and forth, carrying large platters of steaming food to every table. Take a closer look and you will observe that on every table is a round, spinning platform covered with food. It's the lazy Susan, a primary symbol of the Asian feast.

For the Vietnamese, these feasts at fine-dining, lazy Susan–whirling establishments are one of many practices that exemplify our culture and traditions. Family feasts and gatherings are required for weddings and funerals and death anniversaries as well as holidays, such as Tet, the Vietnamese New Year, and Tet Trung Thu, the Mid-Autumn Moon Festival. But even work or school successes are reason enough for a party. Sharing food is the traditional way family and friends celebrate, so naturally a round table is the only shape befitting a group of equals, an important reflection of the Vietnamese culture. Vietnamese beliefs follow yin and yang, and the lazy Susan gives balance to the meal, making it possible to serve all the guests at the table quickly and proportionately.

While typical Vietnamese meals consist of three to five dishes served with large amounts of steamed rice, the salad platter, and dipping sauce, more feasting dishes are served on the lazy Susan. Banquets generally feature three courses with a total of seven or eight dishes—lucky numbers for the Vietnamese. (The numbers seven and eight are symbolic of luck and wealth.) The Chinese believe that the number nine is a good number for relationships; the Vietnamese agree and generally serve nine dishes at a wedding reception. Cold dishes and a sumptuous soup start the three-course meal; the last course is dessert, usually just a plate of cut oranges or a wedding cake. There is some order to how the food is served, but dishes are served so quickly, it seems almost simultaneous. This is done to give a sense of abundance and generosity, putting the host or guest of honor in a good light.

Only the best foods are served, as fine food is a direct reflection of status. You won't find bun, or simple steamed fish, or anything in a clay pot. Beef, poultry (duck is more popular than chicken), and pork are served. Seafood dishes are elaborate and expensive, such as lobster, crab, and an incredibly large whole fish. Fried rice dishes are served in lieu of steamed rice and usually include expensive goodies like dried mushrooms and crabmeat. The feast is also the proper place to incorporate new ingredients and new dishes, so it is only at these restaurants where innovative dishes should be introduced.

A number of the recipes in this chapter will give you an idea of some of the celebratory dishes the Vietnamese enjoy in Little Saigon. Many of the recipes are more traditional, Chinese-style dishes of the Vietnamese feast, but together with some choice dishes from the seafood chapter, you will be ready to prepare your own Vietnamese party at home, based on long-term favorites served on Little Saigon's lazy Susans.

At any large, banquet-scale Vietnamese restaurant, a sign of freshness is the large tank, usually by the front door. It is not a pretty tank, but it is filled with crabs and lobsters. When ordered, a crustacean is taken out of the tank and brought to the diner's table as proof of freshness. This is the kind of pride Vietnamese cooks and restaurateurs take in their ingredients.

PAN-FRIED SPICY CHICKEN WITH MINT AND GINGER
Gà Chiên

In some cuisines, recipes often instruct you to leave the cooking juices behind while you serve the finished product, but this is not the Vietnamese way of doing things. Here's an easy recipe where the chicken is cooked in the marinade and then served with the pan juices instead of with nuoc cham or Maggi sauce. You marinate the chicken overnight to achieve a full, robust flavor, but because the marinade is so potent, you can get away with just 4 hours. Choose breasts or thighs—any part of the chicken you want to cook with. The dish is versatile, so you can grill or bake the marinated chicken, but pan-frying certainly gives it a nice, crispy finish.

6 tablespoons oil

1/2 tablespoon ground white pepper

1/2 onion, finely chopped

5 cloves garlic, finely chopped

1/4 cup chopped fresh Vietnamese
  coriander leaves

1/3 cup roughly chopped fresh
  mint leaves

1 tablespoon chopped fresh ginger

1/4 cup fish sauce

1 fresh Thai bird chile, finely
  chopped

1/2 tablespoon sugar

2 pounds skinless chicken parts

Fresh mint and cilantro leaves
  to garnish

1. First make the marinade. In a large bowl, combine 1 tablespoon of the oil, the white pepper, onion, garlic, coriander leaves, mint leaves, ginger, fish sauce, chile, and sugar. Stir well until the sugar is dissolved.

2. Clean the chicken pieces and pat them dry. Put them in a large bowl or shallow dish and pour the marinade on top. Rub the marinade all over the chicken until each piece is evenly coated. Cover and refrigerate for 4 hours or overnight.

3. Find a frying pan large enough to fit all the chicken pieces in one layer. (If you do not have such a pan, you will need to cook the chicken in two batches.) Pour the remaining oil into the pan over high heat. When the oil is hot, add all the chicken and all the marinade (or half the chicken and half the marinade).

4. Cook the chicken on one side for about 15 minutes, or until it has become golden brown, then turn over and cook the other side for about 15 minutes. Test the chicken for doneness by pricking it with a fork; when the juices run clear, remove the chicken from the pan.

5. Serve the chicken with steamed rice, and garnish with the fresh cilantro and mint leaves. Drizzle the pan juices over the rice.

[SERVES 2]

PAN-FRIED CHICKEN WITH LEMONGRASS, GARLIC, AND CHILI PASTE
Gà Xào Xả Tỏi Ớt

Here's another recipe where the chicken is cooked in the marinade and then the cooking juices are drizzled over steamed rice to eat with the chicken. The difference between this dish and ga chien is the use of lemongrass, which adds zing and fragrance to the chicken. If you have only 4 hours to marinate the chicken, add another 2 tablespoons of fish sauce, but you'll appreciate the dish more if you marinate it overnight. If you prefer more of a kick to the flavors, add extra chili paste, about 1/2 teaspoon.

1/4 cup fish sauce

1 tablespoon sugar

1/2 teaspoon chili paste

1 teaspoon ground black pepper

5 cloves garlic, minced

2 stalks fresh lemongrass, finely chopped

1 1/2 pounds skinless chicken legs and thighs

6 tablespoons oil

1 yellow onion, quartered and separated

Fresh cilantro leaves (or parsley or mint) for garnish

1. In a small bowl, combine the fish sauce, sugar, chili paste, black pepper, garlic cloves, and lemongrass. Whisk until the sugar is completely dissolved.

2. Clean the chicken pieces and pat dry. Put them in a large bowl or shallow dish and pour the marinade on top. Rub the marinade all over the chicken until each piece is evenly coated. Cover and refrigerate overnight.

3. Find a frying pan large enough to fit all the chicken pieces in one layer. (If you do not have such a pan, you will need to cook the chicken in two batches.) Heat the oil in a large frying pan or skillet over high heat. Add the onion and cook for 2 minutes.

4. Add all the chicken and all the marinade (or half the chicken and half the marinade).

5. Cook the chicken on one side for about 15 minutes, or until it has become golden brown, then turn over and cook the other side for about 15 minutes. Test the chicken for doneness by pricking it with a fork; when the juices run clear, remove the chicken from the pan.

6. Serve the chicken with steamed rice and garnish with cilantro. Drizzle the pan juices over the chicken and rice.

[SERVES 4]

FIVE-SPICED CHICKEN
Gà Ngũ Vị Hưởng

Five-spice powder is a magical formula balancing peppercorns, cinnamon, cloves, fennel seeds, and star anise. We credit the Chinese for the invention and use it in many Vietnamese dishes. Five-spiced Chicken is not only flavorful but also aromatic; it's often sold in the meat delis of Little Saigon. But if you want to make it yourself, it's very simple. I prefer to use individual pieces of chicken because it's easier to marinate them thoroughly, but you can certainly apply this recipe to a whole chicken. Because it's not a typical, salty Vietnamese dish, Five-spiced Chicken can be served with fried rice or a sautéed noodle dish.

3 pounds whole chicken, quartered
   and skinless

1 small yellow onion, roughly
   chopped

6 cloves garlic

1/2 tablespoon ground star anise

1 tablespoon sugar

1/3 cup sesame seed oil

2 1/2 tablespoons five-spice powder

1 teaspoon salt

1 teaspoon ground black pepper

3 tablespoons soy sauce

Ginger Lime Soy Sauce (see
   recipe in Basics)

1. Clean and pat dry the chicken quarters. Set aside.

2. In a food processor, mince the onion and garlic. Blend in the ground star anise. Scrape into a small bowl.

3. To the bowl, add the sugar, sesame seed oil, five-spice powder, salt, black pepper, and soy sauce. Whisk until the sugar and salt are dissolved.

4. Place the chicken quarters in a shallow dish or a large ziplock bag. Pour the marinade over the chicken, making sure all parts are completely covered. Marinate for at least 6 hours, but ideally overnight. Every so often, baste the chicken in the dish or rotate the bag to ensure that the chicken parts are always well coated.

5. Prepare a grill for cooking the chicken. A large skillet set on a hot burner is a good alternative. When the grill is hot, place the chicken on it and cook for 10 to 15 minutes on each side, frequently basting the chicken with the marinade. If you are using a skillet, pour all the marinade into the skillet to cook with the chicken. The chicken is cooked when it is pricked with a knife or fork and the juices run clear.

6. Arrange the chicken on a bed of lettuce. Serve hot with Ginger Lime Soy Sauce and steamed or fried rice or sautéed noodles.

[SERVES 4]

FIVE-SPICED FRIED CHICKEN
Gà Chiên Dòn

Fried chicken has found a home in Vietnamese cuisine—but not with the same thick coating found on southern-fried chicken. The Vietnamese version is lightly fried marinated chicken with a coating of five-spice powder and rice flour. The five-spice powder gives the chicken a nice vivid hue, while the rice flour provides a light, crispy crunch. Serve the fried chicken hot from the skillet, with nuoc cham, Ginger Lime Soy Sauce, or just soy sauce. Do not forget the steamed or fried rice and the salad platter. We're still waiting for a Vietnamese version of potato salad and collard greens.

1 whole chicken with skin, cut into 6 pieces

8 cloves garlic, minced

1/2 onion, minced

3 tablespoons soy sauce

3 tablespoons fish sauce

1 tablespoon sugar

2 tablespoons sesame seed oil

2 cups rice flour

1/4 cup five-spice powder

1 tablespoon salt

1 tablespoon black pepper

Oil for frying, approximately 2 cups

1. Wash and pat dry the pieces of chicken. Arrange the pieces in a bowl or a plastic ziplock bag.

2. To make the marinade, in a small bowl combine the garlic and minced onion with the soy sauce, fish sauce, sugar, and sesame seed oil. Stir until the sugar is dissolved.

3. Pour the marinade over the chicken, making sure all parts are completely covered. Cover the bowl or seal the plastic bag, and refrigerate for at least 4 hours or overnight to marinate.

4. In a shallow dish, combine the rice flour, five-spice powder, salt, and pepper thoroughly.

5. Begin heating just 1 cup of oil in a deep skillet or saucepan until it reaches 360 degrees, which is before the oil begins to smoke.

6. While waiting for the oil to heat, take the pieces of chicken out of the marinade one at a time. Dredge each one in the rice flour mixture, giving it a light coating all over. Set aside. Reserve the marinade.

7. When the oil is hot, reduce the heat to medium and fry the chicken for approximately 15 minutes on each side or until it is a golden brown. You do not want to deep-fry the chicken. Test the doneness of the chicken by pricking it with a fork; it is done when the juices run clear. Remove the chicken from the skillet and place on paper towels to soak up the excess oil. Fry the remaining chicken pieces, adding more oil as needed.

8. Serve the chicken over lettuce or watercress with nuoc cham or a soy sauce. Serve with fried or steamed rice and the salad platter.

[SERVES 4]

POACHED GINGER CHICKEN WITH GINGER SAUCE
Gà Siu Siu

Steam a whole chicken? It can be done. For this dish, you want to use a whole chicken, but if you must, you can use chicken quarters as long as you cut the cooking time by a third. Another slow dish, this poached chicken can be started and then left on the back of the stove to continue cooking. It's low-temperature, slow poaching. But the chicken is only half of the dish. The ginger dipping sauce is the crowning touch.

1 whole chicken, about 3 pounds, with bones

4 to 6 cups chicken or vegetable broth

1 medium piece fresh ginger, roughly peeled

1 cup fish sauce

1 onion, quartered

4 cloves garlic, smashed

1 small piece rock sugar (size of a thumb), or 1 tablespoon granulated sugar

2 scallions, roughly chopped

1 teaspoon black peppercorns

Dipping Sauce with Ginger (see recipe in Basics)

1. Clean the chicken and pat it dry. Put it in a large stockpot.

2. Pour the broth over the chicken until just a third of the chicken is covered. If using chicken parts, just stack them on top of each other and pour in 1 to 2 cups of broth.

3. Chop the ginger into a few pieces. Add them to the pot along with the fish sauce, onion, garlic, sugar, scallions, and peppercorns. Stir the ingredients thoroughly into the broth. Bring the broth to a boil; let boil for 5 minutes and then reduce to a simmer.

4. Simmer the pot (do not boil) for 15 minutes, uncovered. Then turn off the heat and flip the chicken over, so that the part of the chicken that was not in the broth is now covered. If using chicken parts, simply rearrange so that the uncooked parts are now submerged in the liquid. Cover the pot and let it sit for about an hour. The chicken will continue cooking even though the heat is turned off. It will be done in about an hour and half, but can continue to sit.

5. You'll know the chicken is done when a fork is poked into the breast and the juices run clear. Remove it from the stockpot and carve it against the grain.

6. Arrange the sliced chicken on a bed of lettuce or watercress on a large serving platter. Spoon a few tablespoons of the poaching liquid over the chicken; discard the rest of the liquid. Serve with hot rice and ginger dipping sauce.

[SERVES 4]

WARM "SHAKING BEEF" SALAD WITH WATERCRESS AND TOMATOES
Bò Lúc Lắc

The English translation of luc lac means "to shake" something, as in some kind of covered container. This is exactly what you need to do with this marinated beef—luc lac it in a container with a lid or in a mixing bowl with a large plate on top. Watercress is a refreshing green, but somewhat bland, so adding this flavorful beef makes for an interesting contrast. If you do not have watercress, try mâche (lamb's lettuce) or red lettuce. The tomatoes are not a must, but they do add taste and color.

1 pound beef (filet or sirloin; best grade recommended)

5 tablespoons olive oil

$1/4$ cup fish sauce

$1/4$ teaspoon salt

1 teaspoon black pepper

2 tablespoons oyster sauce

6 cloves garlic, finely chopped

$1/2$ tablespoons sugar

1 bunch watercress, stems removed, approximately 3 cups

2 large onions, quartered and separated

$1/2$ teaspoon cornstarch

2 large tomatoes, each cut into 6 wedges

1. Slice the beef into $1/2$-inch cubes.

2. Prepare the marinade in a bowl or container with a lid by combining 2 tablespoons of the oil, the fish sauce, salt, black pepper, oyster sauce, garlic, and sugar. Mix well until the sugar is dissolved, then add the beef cubes. Cover the bowl or container and shake the cubes to evenly coat the meat (or you can simply stir). Leave the cover on and let the container sit for 20 minutes on the counter.

3. Clean the watercress and arrange it on a large serving platter or dish.

4. In a large skillet, heat the remaining 3 tablespoons oil over high heat. When it is hot, add the onion. Sauté for just a few minutes, then throw in the beef with its marinade and toss quickly. You need to cook for only 5 minutes over low to medium heat for the meat to be medium rare; continue tossing as it cooks. Cook it longer if you prefer.

5. When the meat is cooked, turn off the burner and stir in the cornstarch to thicken the sauce. Spoon the meat onto the watercress, add tomato wedges, and pour on the cooking juices (as much as you wish). Serve family-style with hot steamed rice.

[SERVES 6]

GRILLED BEEF WITH LEMONGRASS, GARLIC, AND CHILI PASTE
Bò Xào Xả Ớt Tỏi

The flavorful combination of lemongrass, garlic, and chili paste makes a great marinade for sliced beef. Lemongrass is one of those herbs that add an intense flavor to meat. If you do not want to grill the meat, sautéing it with the marinade also creates a delicious dish.

¼ tablespoon salt

½ tablespoon ground black
  pepper

¼ tablespoon sugar

1 teaspoon chili paste

¼ cup fish sauce

1 tablespoon water

2 tablespoons oil

1 large onion, sliced

1 shallot, finely chopped

6 cloves garlic, finely chopped

3 stalks fresh lemongrass, finely
  chopped

1 pound beef (any cut that is not
  too lean: beef round, tenderloin,
  filet), cut into thin slices

Watercress or red lettuce for
  garnish

1 scallion, chopped into rings

Chopped peanuts for garnish

1. In a small bowl, combine the salt, pepper, sugar, chili paste, fish sauce, and water. Whisk until the salt and sugar are dissolved. Set aside.

2. In a medium skillet, heat the oil over high heat. Add the onion and shallot and cook for a few minutes. Next, add the garlic and lemongrass and cook for a minute.

3. Reduce the heat to low and add the beef slices. Quickly pour the fish sauce mixture over the meat. Toss all the ingredients together so that the sauce evenly coats the meat. The meat should cook in the juices for another 5 to 8 minutes for medium rare.

4. Arrange the meat over a bed of watercress or lettuce, and pour the pan juices over the meat. Garnish with the scallions and chopped peanuts. Serve hot with steamed rice or bun.

[SERVES 4]

The majority of Little Saigon's banquet-style restaurants are not on the Bolsa strip but on adjacent streets such as Brookhurst Avenue and Westminster and Garden Grove Boulevards. These restaurants are the only Vietnamese places that have English names, such as Seafood Cove, Capital Seafood, Emerald Palace, and the chain of Seafood Paradise restaurants that are simply numbered 1, 2, and 3. In the evening their focus is on the banquet, but in the morning these same restaurants serve dim sum, a Chinese brunch consisting of endless dumplings and tea.

BEEF TENDERLOIN CURED WITH LIME JUICE AND ONIONS
Bò Tái Chanh

This is the Vietnamese version of beef tartare. To keep the authenticity of the recipe, you will need to use a very high-quality cut of beef. If this is difficult to find (ask your butcher; don't use the plastic-wrapped meat at the supermarket), you can still duplicate this dish by very lightly searing the meat first. Round steak is the meat generally used in Vietnam, but with access to so many great cuts in the United States, we use beef tenderloin here. The meat must be cut into paper-thin slices with your sharpest knife before being marinated in a lime, garlic, and fish sauce combination. This is a popular dish served at nhau, a night of revelry, food, and heavy drinking. A favorite nhau meal is bo bay mon, or "seven courses of beef."

3/4 pound tenderloin

1 large onion, thinly sliced

1/2 cup fresh lime juice

1 teaspoon Sriracha chili sauce

2 tablespoons fish sauce

6 cloves garlic, finely chopped

1/2 teaspoon black pepper

1/2 tablespoon sugar

2 tablespoons olive or vegetable oil for searing

1 cup fresh mung bean sprouts

1 scallion, sliced into rings

3 fresh whole Thai bird chiles for garnish

Fresh cilantro leaves for garnish

1/3 cup crushed unsalted peanuts

1. With your sharpest, thin-blade knife, try your best to slice paper-thin pieces against the grain, if your butcher has not done so. If the meat is very cold, it is easier to handle and to slice. Put the beef into a shallow dish.

2. In a medium bowl, whisk together the onion, lime juice, Sriracha chili sauce, fish sauce, garlic, black pepper, and sugar, until the sugar is completely dissolved. Set the marinade aside.

3. If you're searing the beef, heat a lightly oiled skillet or grill pan over high heat. Put in the slices of raw beef and cook on each side for about 10 seconds each. Transfer from the pan to a clean dish.

4. Pour the marinade all over the raw or seared beef. Make sure the slices are completely coated by tossing the meat together with the marinade. Let sit for 15 minutes in the refrigerator if the beef is raw to allow the lime marinade to "cook" and cure it. If the meat is seared, let it sit for just 5 minutes on the counter.

5. Spoon the sliced beef with the marinade over a bed of mung bean sprouts on a serving platter. Garnish with scallions, whole chile, cilantro, and roasted peanuts. Serve with steamed rice and the salad platter and a bowl of nuoc cham.

[SERVES 4]

PAN-FRIED FILET OF BEEF WITH TOMATO AND HERBS
Bò Bít Tết

This dish is always a favorite at wedding receptions. The sweet and salty marinade creates a lusty meat that is almost buttery in texture and flavor. With the fresh tomatoes and herbs, the dish comes out light and clean. The meat is best suited for pan-frying, as the residual juices and marinade can be tossed in the skillet together with the tomatoes and herbs for added flavor. Grilling is a satisfactory variation.

2 tablespoons fish sauce

1/2 tablespoon fresh lime juice

1/2 fresh Thai bird chile, finely chopped

1/2 tablespoon sugar

1/2 tablespoon black pepper

1/4 cup roughly chopped fresh mint leaves

1/4 cup roughly chopped fresh cilantro leaves

1/4 cup roughly chopped fresh Vietnamese coriander leaves

1/4 cup roughly chopped fresh Thai basil leaves

2 scallions, chopped into rings

2 tablespoons oil

2 shallots, diced

3 cloves garlic, finely chopped

1 pound filet mignon, cut into 1/2-inch-thick slices

3 medium tomatoes, each cut into 6 pieces

1/2 small cucumber, peeled and thinly sliced

1. In a small bowl, whisk together the fish sauce, lime juice, chile, sugar, and black pepper, until the sugar is dissolved.

2. In a large bowl, toss together the mint, cilantro, coriander, Thai basil, and scallions. Sprinkle them over a large platter.

3. In a large skillet, heat the oil over high heat. Add the shallots and cook for a few minutes, then add the garlic and cook for another minute.

4. Add the sliced filet to the pan. Pour the fish sauce mixture over it and toss quickly. Reduce the heat to medium and cook for a minute before adding the tomatoes and sliced cucumber. Cook for another 3 to 4 minutes for medium rare.

5. Arrange the beef, tomatoes, and cucumber over the herbs. Top with the liquid from the skillet. Serve immediately with hot steamed rice or plain bun.

[SERVES 2]

RICE NOODLES STIR-FRIED WITH VEGETABLES, PORK, AND SHRIMP
Hủ Tiếu Xào Tom Thịt

This is a great, family-style noodle dish to serve as either a side dish or a main course at a large dinner. Hu tieu noodles are great, flat noodles that are fun to eat. With large, stir-fried noodle dishes, it is always nice to offer a few dishes of sauces so that diners can flavor the noodles to their own liking. For example, try serving this dish with nuoc cham, Peanut Sauce (see recipe in Basics), or Maggi. Or try a different type of noodle—egg or thin rice vermicelli (bun). Substitute pork for beef or chicken, or go vegetarian with tofu or bean curd. You can also add more vegetables to the stir-fry.

1/3 pound lean pork shoulder

1 1/2 tablespoons fish sauce

1 tablespoon soy sauce

2 tablespoons oyster sauce

1/2 teaspoon chili paste

1/2 tablespoon black pepper

1/2 tablespoon sugar

3 tablespoons sesame seed oil

1 large onion, diced

2 shallots, diced

5 cloves garlic, smashed

1/2 pound raw fresh shrimp, peeled, deveined, and cut lengthwise

2 medium carrots, julienned and cut into 2-inch pieces

1 stalk celery, roughly chopped

1 cup chopped bok choy

1 cup broccoli florets

6 cups cooked wide rice noodles

2 scallions, chopped into rings

1. Slice the pork into very thin slices, and then cut those slices into 2x1-inch pieces.

2. In a small bowl, whisk together the fish sauce, soy sauce, oyster sauce, chili paste, black pepper, and sugar, until the sugar is dissolved. Set aside.

3. In a large skillet or wok, heat the oil over medium heat. When it is hot, sauté the onions and shallots for about 5 minutes. Add the garlic cloves and continue cooking for another 3 minutes.

4. Add the sliced pork and cook for about 8 minutes or until it is no longer pink. Add the shrimp and cook for about 3 minutes or until it has curled and turned pink in color.

5. Add the carrots, celery, bok choy, and broccoli florets to the skillet and cook for about 5 minutes.

6. Finally, add the noodles and the fish sauce mixture and quickly sauté the noodles for another minute. Turn off the heat and continue tossing all the ingredients until they are evenly blended and distributed.

7. Add the scallions and serve on a large platter.

[SERVES 6]

GINGERED SAUTEED EGG NOODLES WITH PORK, SHRIMP, AND VEGETABLES
Mì Xào Dòn

This is not the bird's-nest fried noodle dish that we see so often at Chinese and Vietnamese restaurants. Rather than deep-frying the noodles, this recipe is light on oil and has great flavors from myriad ingredients. Substitute or add tofu or any other ingredients you enjoy. The seafood version of this dish consists of just shrimp, squid, and vegetables. But the beauty of this recipe is adding what you please.

1/2 pound pork shoulder (or another fatty pork meat like bacon)

1/4 cup fish sauce

1 teaspoon chili paste

3 tablespoons oyster sauce

1 tablespoon ground black pepper

5 tablespoons oil

1 large onion, diced

2 shallots, diced

8 cloves garlic, finely chopped

1 tablespoon finely chopped fresh ginger

1 medium carrot, julienned

1 small bunch broccoli, rinsed and separated

1/3 pound raw fresh shrimp, peeled and deveined

1 cup snow peas

1 bunch bok choy, roughly chopped

1/3 cup straw mushrooms

6 cups cooked thin or thick egg noodles

2 scallions, chopped into rings

1/4 cup fresh cilantro leaves

1/3 cup chopped unsalted dry-roasted peanuts

1. Cut the pork into bite-size, 1/4-inch-thick slices. Prepare all the remaining ingredients before you start stir-frying and arrange them separately near your stove.

2. In a small bowl, whisk together the fish sauce, chili paste, oyster sauce, and pepper.

3. In a large skillet or wok, heat the oil over medium heat. When it is hot, add the onions and shallots and cook for about 3 minutes or until brown. Add the garlic and cook for another few minutes.

4. Add the ginger, then the carrots, pork, and broccoli. Cook and stir quickly for a few minutes. Then add the fish sauce combination and blend well.

5. After 5 minutes, or when the broccoli begins to soften, add the shrimp, snow peas, bok choy, and mushrooms. Cook for another 2 minutes or until the shrimp and pork are cooked.

6. Add the cooked noodles and scallions and blend evenly.

7. Serve hot on a large platter, garnished with the cilantro and crushed peanuts.

[SERVES 4]

TRADITIONAL FRIED RICE
Cơm Chiên Tom Cải

There is always leftover steamed rice from past dinners, but what to do with it? Recycle it into flavorful fried rice! Traditional Vietnamese fried rice is often served as an entree on the lazy Susan in Little Saigon's restaurants. And at elaborate wedding dinners, our fried rice often includes bits of crab and even lobster. A heaping plate of fried rice should not be served with salty main dishes, as it is already seasoned and salted. If you have been eager to use your wok, here is your chance, but a large, deep skillet is perfectly appropriate as well. Once you have the idea of this basic recipe, add more of your favorite ingredients—substitute tofu for the sausage, add broccoli or bok choy—any way you like.

6 cups cooked and cooled
   white rice

4 large eggs

1/4 cup fish sauce

1 teaspoon chili paste

1 tablespoon oyster sauce

1 1/2 teaspoons ground black
   pepper

1 tablespoon sugar

1/4 cup olive oil

1 large onion, diced

4 cloves garlic, finely chopped

1 cup fresh mung bean sprouts

2 large carrots, diced

1 cup frozen or canned peas

1 cup snow peas

2 Chinese sausages, cut lengthwise and diced

2 scallions, sliced into rings

1/2 pound raw shrimp, peeled,
   and sliced lengthwise

1 tablespoon Maggi Seasoning Sauce

1/2 cup roughly chopped fresh cilantro leaves

Chopped unsalted dry-roasted peanuts (optional)

1. Put the rice in a large bowl. Break apart any clumps with your hands or a fork. Then crack the eggs over the rice and stir to combine. Each grain of rice does not need to be evenly coated with egg.

2. In a small bowl, combine the fish sauce, chili paste, oyster sauce, black pepper, and sugar, and whisk until the sugar is dissolved.

3. Prepare all your ingredients and arrange them separately near the stove. If you are using a wok, you can make the entire recipe at one time, but if you have only a large skillet, divide the ingredients in half to cook two batches.

4. Begin by heating the oil over high heat. When the oil is hot, bring the heat down to medium and add the onions. Cook until soft or about 5 minutes. Then add the garlic and cook for another minute. Add the bean sprouts, carrots, peas, and snow peas and cook until they are soft, about 3 minutes. It is important that you constantly stir the ingredients as they cook. Add the fish sauce mixture. Stir well.

5. Add the sausage, scallions, and shrimp, and continue stirring for another 5 minutes until the shrimp is cooked through. Finally add the rice and stir quickly for about a minute to make sure everything is tossed together evenly.

6. Pour the Maggi sauce over everything and toss further just to combine.

7. Transfer to a large serving plate or bowl, and garnish with more black pepper, cilantro, and, if desired, the roasted peanuts.

[SERVES 6]

Festive Holiday Foods

TET, THE VIETNAMESE NEW YEAR

Tet, short for "Tet Nguyen Dan," is the Vietnamese New Year, and by far the most celebrated and festive of holidays for the Vietnamese and the Little Saigon community. Tet is based on specific moon calculations on the lunar calendar and generally takes place in late January or early February, on the same day as the Chinese New Year. The holiday, which starts on Tet and continues for two more days, is rooted in centuries-old traditions, with a special emphasis on food and feasting. Families congregate, most people attend temple or church, schools and businesses have time off, and numerous festivals are held.

For many Vietnamese Americans all over the country, Tet involves a pilgrimage to Little Saigon, because of its many festivities and large concentration of Buddhist temples. The cities of Westminster and Garden Grove see more tourists during the Tet season than at any other time of the year. More than just encompassing the spirit and excitement of a new year, recent Tet festivities in Little Saigon have become more focused on passing on the core cultural traditions of Tet to the next generation. In the early 1980s celebrations involved just a dragon dance or a tiny community parade, but today there are plays based on Vietnamese mythology put on by local Vietnamese student organizations, entire replicas of rural Vietnam, pageants, extravagant Vietnamese music shows, as well as dragon dances, firecrackers, orchids, and cherry blossom stands. Tet festival proceeds go on to fund community programs and projects for the rest of the year.

Leading up to Tet, families spend days cleaning and preparing their homes in anticipation of the festivities. Homes are decorated, new clothes purchased, and bills and debts settled in order to begin the new year with a clean slate. In present-day Little Saigon, the community shuts down early on Tet, rather than take the whole day off, which still allows for family time and traditions such as the giving of li si to children. The family congregates—usually in a grandparent's or another elder's home (showing respect by visiting the eldest in the family)—and the children take their turn saying a chuc Tet, or wish, to each adult, perhaps "Chuc cau, vui ve, manh khoe cho nam moi," or "I wish Uncle happiness, health in this new year." So pleased is Uncle with this greeting that he grants each child a red li si, stuffed with new bills. The same routine continues with each adult relative. Thus, capitalism and enterpreneurial skills are taught to children at a young age as they gather all those red money envelopes from their relatives. (The color red stands for wealth and prosperity, and during Tet the streets of Little Saigon are draped with red ribbon.)

The Vietnamese call celebrating Tet *an Tet,* which translates verbatim as "eating Tet." It is appropriate, given that the holiday revolves around the celebration of food and its consumption. The business of food is of great importance during Tet; restaurants participate as vendors at festivals, or remain in their locations and brace themselves for the influx of tourists and celebrants. The elaborate and abundant meals also occur at the homes of friends and family. The foods have to be made in advance and must be able to be kept for several days simply because people are too busy celebrating during Tet to do any cooking.

The traditional foods of Tet vary from one region to another in Vietnam. In the North there are jellied meats, salted carp, and boiled chicken. In Central Vietnam, or Hue, there are more meat dishes and shrimp pies. In the South, where it is much warmer, there is more emphasis on thit kho—foods slowly braised with lots of fish sauce and coconut juice. Salting meats keeps the foods preserved for much longer in a land of no refrigeration. The beauty of kho dishes is that they taste even better the next day.

Besides the regional dishes, there are a number of other Tet treats (such as banh Tet, banh day, and banh trung, all made of pork and a green mung bean paste in a glutinous rice shell, and wrapped in banana leaves that give the banh its green coloring when steamed) and assortments of different candied coconut, peanut brittle, dates, and fruits that are given to family and neighbors. These traditional Tet foods are now mostly purchased instead of being made at home. Nuts and candied fruits are boxed and sold in ornate red tins. It's part of the holiday commercialism that has evolved in Little Saigon. Whether this is a positive or negative trend, it does leave more time for many to participate in the revelry and the celebrations within the community.

What specifically do the Vietnamese eat at home, at the festivals, and in the restaurants during this festive season? In this chapter you will find the more popular Tet dishes of the South Vietnamese such as kho and other braised foods, and festive dishes for a large party. The Lazy Susan chapter provides even more recipes for the celebratory New Year's dinners served by many of the restaurants during the Tet season. Many of these recipes you will want to serve year-round.

PORK BRAISED IN CARAMEL SAUCE
Thịt Kho

The Vietnamese are known for kho dishes—braised, caramelized food. When sugar is cooked over medium to high heat, it will caramelize into a thick brown sauce. Some cooks like to create a caramel sauce to pour over the food. I prefer to cover the meat with a generous amount of sugar and brown it, which produces a nice caramel coating as well as permeating the food with a light taste of sugar. As the meat braises, the liquid and sugars will continue to cook and thicken. *Kho* is a verb, and it explains the process of slowly braising foods with lots of fish sauce and coconut juice.

This slow-cooked braised pork in coconut juice has a wonderful caramel sauce and is one of my maternal grandma's (ba ngoai) best dishes. Some may find cooking with the fat and rind of the pork unappealing, but braising with the fat makes for a more flavorful dish. However, you can certainly make this dish with other pork cuts, such as pork spareribs or leaner pork cuts like sirloin or tenderloin; just keep the pieces in bite-size portions.

2 hard-boiled eggs

1/2 pound pork shoulder, with fat and rind (or slab bacon)

2 1/2 tablespoons sugar

1/3 cup fish sauce

1 1/2 cups fresh coconut juice or coconut soda such as Coco Rico

1 scallion, chopped into rings

1/2 tablespoon ground black pepper

1. Peel the eggs and set them aside.

2. Cut the pork into large, 2-inch cubes, cutting against the grain, so that each piece includes the lean meat, fat, and rind. Pat dry.

3. In a clay pot or saucepan, caramelize the sugar until brown.

4. Add the pork and toss.

5. Add the fish sauce and stir the cubes to evenly cover them. Then add 1/3 cup of the coconut juice or soda and bring the pot to a boil. Let it boil for 5 minutes, then lower the heat to a simmer.

6. Cover the pot and let it simmer for 30 minutes. Then add the hard-boiled eggs and the remainder of the coconut soda and simmer for an hour, or until the meat is tender.

7. The dish is ready once the liquid has been reduced to a liquidy, brown sauce. The pork and eggs should be a light brown color, and the pork should be extremely tender.

8. Garnish with the scallions and ground black pepper and serve with hot rice.

[SERVES 4]

Asians love pickling, salt-curing, and fermenting eggs. From marbled eggs to the 1,000-year-old egg, the Chinese have created many recipes to celebrate the egg's symbolism of fertility and rebirth. The Vietnamese are no different. They salt and ferment hard-boiled eggs, and in this recipe they braise them along with the pork. The entire egg turns brown in color and is salted all the way to the yolk. Like other salted or pickled eggs, braised eggs from the kho dish are shared by either cutting them into wedges before serving, or letting diners eat them directly from the pot by breaking and sharing them with chopsticks.

CHICKEN BRAISED IN GINGER AND COCONUT
Gà Kho Gừng

On a gloomy day, coming home to this braised chicken dish is better than money in the bank. The chicken is very flavorful and moist, and it falls straight off the bone. It's perfect with some plain steamed rice over which you've drizzled the caramel braising sauce.

1½ to 2 pounds chicken thighs
   and legs, skinless
3 cloves garlic, finely chopped
¼ cup fish sauce
1 teaspoon ground black pepper
2 scallions, sliced into rings
1 tablespoon olive oil
3 tablespoons minced fresh ginger
½ fresh Thai bird chile, chopped
   into rings
2 tablespoons sugar
2 cups fresh coconut juice or
   coconut soda such as Coco Rico
Fresh cilantro

1. Clean the chicken pieces and pat dry.

2. In a small bowl, combine the garlic, fish sauce, black pepper, scallions, 1 tablespoon of the olive oil, the ginger, and chile.

3. In a clay pot or saucepan, caramelize the sugar until brown. Add the chicken and coat with caramel.

4. Pour the fish sauce mixture all over the chicken. Add just ½ cup of the coconut juice or soda and gently stir it in. Bring the pot to a boil and let it continue to boil for 10 to 15 minutes. Add remainder of coconut juice or soda. Lower the heat to a simmer and cover the pot.

5. Continue simmering the chicken for 2 hours, or until liquid has reduced to half.

6. After 2 hours, the chicken will be thoroughly cooked, and the meat will be falling off the bone. The sauce will have thickened nicely. If you prefer a more syrupy texture, you can continue cooking, but for no longer than 30 minutes. Either way, serve the chicken with hot rice. Drizzle the sauce over the rice and garnish with fresh cilantro and black pepper.

[SERVES 4]

A CELEBRATION FOR THE CHILDREN

The Mid-Autumn Moon Festival, Tet Trung Thu, has been important to families in Vietnam for many years, as it is a celebration for the children. It is customarily held on the fifteenth day of the eighth lunar month in late August or early September. The festival originated because parents needed to make up time they'd lost with their children during harvest season. The festival takes place during a full moon and pays homage to it, a symbolic representation of fullness and the prosperity of life.

Children parade on the streets in costumes while singing and carrying colorful lanterns of different sizes. Part of the tradition is for parents to help children make their lanterns and costumes. I remember my mom making our lanterns from printed wrapping paper. She was so meticulous with crimping the paper to make the round lanterns.

Today Tet Trung Thu festivals in Little Saigon continue celebrating children and promoting education,

Saigon, 1957

poetry, dance, and arts and crafts. For food, it is customary to give banh trung thu, boxes of mooncakes, which are traditionally very rich in taste. The cakes are filled with lotus seeds, ground beans, and orange peels and have a bright egg yolk in the center to represent the moon. The cakes are generally sold throughout Little Saigon only on the days leading up to the festival.

CATFISH BRAISED IN CARAMEL SAUCE
Cá Kho Tộ

Ca kho to has always been a traditional recipe of South Vietnam. Because this dish can be made ahead of time, and the saltiness helps it last a little bit longer than your average leftover, it is extremely popular to have during the week of Tet. This version is my grandma's recipe and better than other ca kho to recipes I have had in restaurants. She loves using lots of pepper and keeping the sauce thin. In this recipe, coconut soda or a 7Up-like soda helps break down the proteins of the fish; the carbonated beverage also cuts the fishy smell a little better than coconut juice would. Choose fresh catfish, cod, halibut, or another non-oily fish with a firm flesh. If you use a fish with a soft flesh, such as flounder, the fish will be braised into a puree. It is important that you ask for a cross-sectional cut; better yet, a cut toward the tail where you will find most of the meat. Serve this fish with lots of freshly ground black pepper and steamed white rice.

3/4 pound fresh catfish, cod, or
    halibut, cut in 1-inch cross-
    sectional slices, with skin and
    bones intact (ask your fish-
    monger to do this for you)
2 1/2 tablespoons sugar
1/4 cup fish sauce
1 fresh Thai bird chile, sliced into
    rings with seeds
1 tablespoon ground black pepper
2 cups Coco Rico coconut soda, or
    7Up or similar soda
1 scallion, chopped into rings
Fresh cilantro

1.   Begin by cleaning the fish slices thoroughly. Pat dry and place in a shallow dish.

2.   In a clay pot or saucepan, caramelize the sugar until brown, then place the fish slices in the pot and cover with the caramel sauce. Add the fish sauce, chile, and black pepper; raise the heat to high and cook for another 5 minutes.

3.   Add 1/2 cup of the coconut soda and cook over high heat for a few more minutes before reducing the heat to a simmer. Add remaining soda.

4.   In about 1 hour the finished sauce should have a light syrupy consistency, not too thick. It depends on your preference, but either way, you will have a nice fragrant sauce with the cooked fish.

5.   Serve directly from the clay pot and sprinkle black pepper for garnish over the dish along with the chopped scallion and cilantro. Serve with plenty of steamed rice.

[SERVES 4]

BRAISED DUCK WITH COCONUT JUICE
Vịt Kho Dùa

This is a great dish to introduce to your friends who are having duck for the first time. Though this recipe is similar to the braised chicken dish, duck is a much more succulent and savory meat. With the five-spice powder flavoring and perfuming the duck, you end up with a particularly decadent meal with a delicious, caramelized coconut sauce.

1½ to 2 pounds skinless duck
   thighs and legs
2 tablespoons five-spice powder
4 cloves garlic, finely chopped
¼ cup fish sauce
1 teaspoon ground black pepper
2 scallions, sliced into rings
1 tablespoon oil
1 tablespoon minced fresh ginger
1 fresh Thai bird chile, chopped
   into rings
2 tablespoons sugar
2 cups coconut juice or coconut
   soda such as Coco Rico
Fresh cilantro

1. In a shallow dish or on a baking sheet, arrange the duck thighs and legs and sprinkle five-spice powder over them.

2. In a small bowl, combine the garlic, fish sauce, pepper, scallions, oil, the ginger, and chile.

3. In a clay pot or saucepan, caramelize the sugar until brown. Add the duck and toss in and cover with the caramel.

4. Pour the fish sauce mixture into the pot and gently stir so that it covers all the meat. Add ½ cup coconut juice or soda to the pot, stir, and bring to a boil. Let boil for 15 minutes, then lower the heat to a simmer. As the sauce reduces, add the remaining coconut juice or soda and continue simmering for another 2 hours. For the final product, the sauce should be thick and the duck meat falling off the bone when you serve it.

5. Serve the duck directly from the clay pot, family-style, with hot steamed rice. Drizzle the sauce over the rice for an even better taste. Garnish with the fresh cilantro and additional black pepper.

[SERVES 4]

Tom Sườn Ram Mận

Riblets are like cross-sectional cuts of pork spare ribs. If you don't like shrimp, try the salted short ribs recipe instead. Pay attention to the caramelization process; you don't want to overcook and dry out the riblets. When done correctly, you will have falling-off-the-bone tender meat. It's great to use fatty portions of the riblets, as they can be so unctuous and flavorful. Consider adding shiitake mushrooms to the clay pot; they are great when braised with rich meats like these riblets. Serve with lots of hot steamed rice. This is a salty dish.

1 tablespoon salt

1 1/2 cups water

1/2 pound fresh shrimp, heads removed, shells intact, and deveined

3/4 pound pork riblets

2 tablespoons sugar

1/3 cup fish sauce

1/2 fresh Thai bird chile, finely chopped

5 cloves garlic, finely chopped

1 1/2 teaspoons ground black pepper

2 tablespoons oil

1 medium onion, quartered and separated

3/4 cup fresh shiitake mushrooms (optional)

Fresh cilantro

Chopped scallions

1. In a small bowl, dissolve the salt in the water. Add the shrimp and let it soak in the salt water for an hour. Drain the shrimp and pat dry.

2. In a shallow dish, combine the pork riblets and shrimp. Sprinkle the sugar all over them. Set aside for at least 15 minutes or up to 30 minutes.

3. In a small bowl, stir together the fish sauce, chile, garlic, and black pepper.

4. In a clay pot or saucepan, heat the oil over medium heat. When it is hot, sauté the onions for 5 minutes. Then add the sugared shrimp and pork. Sear the meat and shrimp for about 10 minutes. The sugar should caramelize and turn the meat and shrimp a golden brown.

5. Pour the fish sauce mixture over the shrimp and pork, add the optional shiitake mushrooms, cover the pot, and simmer for a half hour. The fish sauce mixture should be reduced by half.

6. Garnish with cilantro and scallions and serve hot with loads of steamed rice.

[SERVES 4]

Sườn Kho Mận

I could dine happily on this savory dish alone. It is one of my favorites. The sugar and salt in the marinade cure the meat. I love the residual thick sauce because I can pour it over my steamed rice. In a departure from other clay pot dishes, 7Up or Sprite is used here instead of Coco Rico. The soda is a must as it works as a meat tenderizer as well as helping to retain moisture in the meat. Don't be too concerned with the amount of salt; you should serve this dish with copious amounts of steamed rice.

1 pound beef short ribs (pork
   riblets can be substituted)

3 tablespoons sugar

1 teaspoon salt

1/3 cup fish sauce

1 fresh Thai bird chile, finely
   chopped

1/2 tablespoon ground black
   pepper

3 tablespoons oil

2 large shallots, diced

6 cloves garlic, finely chopped

1/2 teaspoon whole cloves

1/2 cup 7Up, Sprite, or generic
   equivalent

1. Pat the short ribs dry and place them in a large bowl or on a shallow dish.

2. In a small bowl, combine the sugar, salt, fish sauce, chile, and pepper. Whisk until the sugar and salt are dissolved. Pour the marinade all over the short ribs, cover, and refrigerate overnight.

3. In a clay pot or a saucepan, heat the oil over medium heat for a few minutes. Sauté the shallots, garlic, and cloves. Add the short ribs with the marinade and sear for about 8 minutes until they are brown on all sides.

4. Add the 7Up or Sprite and cover the pot. Cook for an hour over low heat or until the short ribs are tender and the meat falls off the bone. The liquid should have reduced to a syrup.

5. Serve with loads of hot steamed rice and the salad platter.

[SERVES 4]

Bánh Xèo

Traditionally South Vietnamese fare, these yellow crepes, made with bits of pork, shrimp, mushrooms, and green onions and filled with bean sprouts, are best served when they emerge hot and crispy from the skillet. Alone the blend may seem a bit bland, but once nuoc cham is added, the flavors immediately brighten. It takes some practice to get the crepe to fold over nicely without falling apart. Even if you don't get it right on the first try, a broken crepe is still as delicious to eat as a beautifully presented one. The key to this crepe recipe is the coconut juice, which gives the crepe its rich flavor; don't make the mistake of following a recipe that allows you to substitute something like water or milk for this crucial ingredient. For the filling, pork shoulder is the best choice, but firm tofu, chicken breast, or ground pork or beef can be used as substitutes; just make sure you are using fillings that are firm when cooked, and which do not require much time to cook.

FILLING:

3/4 pound pork shoulder, sliced thin

3 tablespoons salt

8 tablespoons canola oil

2 yellow onions, sliced in rings or
   diced to your own preference

2 cloves garlic, finely chopped

3/4 pound shrimp, halved, peeled,
   and deveined

2 cups thinly sliced white or brown
   mushrooms

1 pound fresh mung bean sprouts

CREPES:

1 1/2 cups water

1 cup coconut milk

2 1/2 cups rice flour

1/2 tablespoon cornstarch

1 tablespoon ground turmeric

1/2 teaspoon salt

4 scallions, sliced thinly into rings

Banks in Little Saigon have become involved in Tet celebrations, passing out red envelopes with bank logos when the Vietnamese go to get fresh new currency for li si. The Wells Fargo Bank has even added the Vietnamese language to their ATM machines and marketing literature.

1. In a large stockpot, boil the pork shoulder for about 20 minutes in water with the 3 tablespoons of salt. When the pork is cooked through, remove it from the pot, pat dry, and set aside to cool. Slice the cooled pork into 1/4-inch slices against the grain. Cover and set aside.

2. Next, prepare the crepe batter. In a large mixing bowl, blend together the water and coconut milk. With a whisk or wooden spoon, slowly add the rice flour and continue stirring to fully blend the dry ingredients into the liquid. Repeat the same procedure as you add the cornstarch, turmeric, and salt. Blend well, as the rice flour tends to collect at the bottom of the bowl. Add the scallions and let the batter sit for 15 minutes.

3. When you are ready to cook the crepes, lay out the crepe filling ingredients next to the stove: canola oil, onions, garlic, shrimp, mushrooms, bean sprouts, and sliced pork. Begin by heating 1 tablespoon of the oil in a 12-inch, nonstick skillet on high heat. Add a few slices of the onions and a pinch of chopped garlic. When sizzling, add 4 or 5 pieces of shrimp, 6 or 7 pieces of the sliced pork, and a small handful of mushrooms. Sauté for a few minutes or until the shrimp is cooked through, curled, and turned pink.

4. Spread the ingredients evenly in the skillet. Add 1/3 cup of the batter and swirl to evenly distribute and cover the surface. The skillet should have a light coating of batter; the sautéed ingredients should not be swimming around in the batter. Adjust the heat to low and cover the skillet.

5. After 3 to 5 minutes, the crepe should be a nice, bright yellow and look cooked, with its outside edges crispy and pulling in from the side. Add 1/8 of the bean sprouts to just one side of the crepe and cook for another minute. Check to see if the crepe is finished by sliding your spatula under part of it and looking at the crispness of the bottom.

6. Once the bottom is crisp, fold the crepe in half to cover the bean sprouts and slide directly onto a large plate. Serve immediately with the salad platter and nuoc cham.

[MAKES 8 CREPES]

Desserts, Savory Treats, and Drinks

BAKERIES AND COFFEEHOUSES

Little Saigon is a place that celebrates food aromas, and on a typical morning the fragrance of freshly ground coffee from coffeehouses and freshly baked bread from bakeries wafts through the air along Bolsa Avenue. It could be said that this is no different from any U.S. city street where bakeries and coffeehouses are commonplace. But there's nothing typical about these Little Saigon destinations. The bakeries here sell baguettes, cakes, and croissants along with traditional Vietnamese che, holiday mooncakes, and the Vietnamese sandwiches called banh mi thit. The coffeehouses aren't simply for coffee and tea and reading; they also sell drinks such as sugarcane juice and soybean milk and during the evening are transformed into cafes with alcoholic beverages, dancing, and singing. Clearly you're a long way from Dunkin' Donuts and Starbucks.

The influence of the French is very strong in Little Saigon bakeries as well as coffeehouses. Using large French-made machines such as the Pavailler automated oven, bakeries are now capable of producing almost 500 loaves of bread an hour. They do make French wheat flour baguettes, but it's the Vietnamese baguettes that sell out. This airy bread used for banh mi thit has a perfect crumbly crust that cracks open to a buttery light dough. The secret ingredient is rice flour, which makes breads that are more airy and less dense than your traditional French bread. However, the addition of rice flour also means the bread won't last as long, and it will get quite stale when left out for more than a day.

Coffee is another import from the French. The Vietnamese have taken this staple, made it more potent, and sweetened it to their liking. They call it cafe sua da.

The coffee requires a special filter that sits on top of a cup or glass filled with some sweetened condensed milk. The espresso-bean grounds or dark-roasted Vietnamese grounds are added to the filter, and then boiling water is poured over the grounds. It takes a few minutes for the strong espresso to drip into the glass. The longer you brew the coffee, the more caffeinated and potent it becomes. Many shops will have glasses of the coffee premade and ready to go.

On a typical Saturday morning in Little Saigon, the lines are out the door at the bakeries. Once you are finally inside, you find yourself in a crowded space with everyone yelling out their orders for banh mi thit, fresh baguettes, cream puffs, tapiocas, and so on. Language is not necessary; point to the displayed item, show the quantity needed with your fingers, and a price will be shouted back to you. On top of the glass display of French pastries and cakes rests a selection of Vietnamese desserts; if it's holiday time, you'll find all the festive treats like mooncakes (banh trung thu) and other pastries stuffed with sweet lotus seeds or red beans.

Because few of the bakeries offer any kind of seating area, most people take their purchases to the nearby coffeehouses, where they can enjoy their treats with some cafe sua da, meet with old friends, and read the Vietnamese newspapers. Elderly gentlemen spend hours sipping their strong, hot, ginger or chrysanthemum teas around a game of Chinese checkers or chess. Plain, herbal teas like tra da or iced green tea are also popular on a hot day. Fruit shakes, or sinh-tos, are especially popular. You can buy canned coconut soda (Coco Rico), guava juice, and a variety of other canned Thai teas and coffees. Nuoc mia, or sugarcane juice, is one of the most popular drinks around and very refreshing. It is not as sweet as you would imagine, but it certainly has a distinct, flowery flavor. In contrast is the Vietnamese variation on lemonade called chanh muoi, which is salted fresh lemonade. Sua dau nanh, or soybean milk, is often served hot or cold, with or without sugar.

By evening the coffeehouses become more like bars. Many have liquor licenses and can sell beer and cocktails. For the younger generation, a lack of activities in Little Saigon means these cafes are a natural destination for music, singing, and dancing. Loud Vietnamese and American pop songs and karaoke, disco balls hanging from the ceilings, and wall-to-wall mirrors are common elements. Owners are under strict ordinance, however, to send patrons under eighteen home by 10:00 P.M., ban smoking, and close at midnight.

The recipes in this chapter give you a hint of the bounty of wonderful treats enjoyed in Little Saigon. Not only will you find noted Vietnamese desserts and beverages, but you will also get a glimpse of the European influence on the cuisine of this Southeast Asian country.

A number of bakeries are not to be missed when visiting Little Saigon. For che and banh mi sandwiches and baguettes, you must go to one of the Che Cali chains. For elaborate and delicate pastries, go to Lily's Bakery, where you'll find pastry so light it crumbles at a glance and does an excellent job of melding Vietnamese flavors into the styles of the French—try jackfruit cake with mango frosting or pineapple and coconut tarts. Van's Bakery and Song Long are the authority for birthday cakes and larger orders of Vietnamese delicacies; they were two of the first bakeries in Little Saigon.

Pâté Châud

These are not the puff pastries of fancy Parisian bakeries; these are meat-filled pastries that are sold in every Little Saigon bakery. Pate chaud is a French creation, but it has become so popular with the Vietnamese that they have made it their own. The meat in the pastry is similar to meat stuffed in other Vietnamese treats. Just ask for the ba-tay show (the *p* is pronounced like *b*; there's no *p* sound in the Vietnamese language). Over the years the pastries have gotten bigger and bigger as bakeries compete for business. After you try this wonderful French-Vietnamese pastry, you will no longer think that puff pastry dough is exclusively for desserts.

$1/3$ pound ground pork

$1/4$ yellow onion, minced

2 cloves garlic, minced

$1/2$ tablespoon ground black pepper

1 teaspoon fish sauce

2 10x12-inch puff pastry sheets, approximately $1/4$ inch thick (frozen Pepperidge Farm puff pastry sheets work well)

2 eggs

1. In a large bowl, combine the ground pork, minced onion, and garlic with your hands. Mix in the pepper and fish sauce. Form meatballs approximately $1 1/2$ inches in diameter. Set aside. Preheat the oven to 400 degrees.

2. Thaw the puff pastry sheets according to package instructions. Sprinkle some flour on a wooden board or countertop.

3. Leave one pastry sheet in the refrigerator while you lay the other sheet on your working surface. With your eyes or a ruler, divide the pastry sheet into nine equal squares, each one $3 1/3$ by 4 inches.

4. Put a meatball in the center of each pastry square. Lightly flatten the meatball with your fingers. Take the second pastry sheet from the refrigerator and gently place it on top of the meatballs, aligning it with the bottom sheet.

5. With a knife or ravioli cutter, cut out the squares. Lightly seal the sides of the squares with your fingertips, about $3/4$ inch from the outside. Place the pastries on a baking sheet lined with parchment paper. It is important that the pastry bottom is placed flat on the sheet pan.

6. Prepare an egg wash by beating the eggs lightly. With a cooking brush, brush the top of each pastry.

7. Bake for 20 minutes or until the pastries are golden brown and have completely puffed. Serve warm.

[MAKES 9 PASTRIES]

TARO ROOT AND GLUTINOUS RICE IN COCONUT MILK
Chè Khoai Môn

Both taro root and glutinous rice have a starchy consistency, which serves as a base for many desserts and tapiocas. Glutinous rice is like a sweet rice flour made from short-grain rice. It becomes moist and sticky when cooked, creating a chewy texture that makes it great as a base for Vietnamese desserts and snacks like che. If my family is cooking taro root for dinner, a few extra roots will always be purchased to make che in the morning to serve hot for breakfast.

½ pound taro root, approximately
   5 small roots

½ cup glutinous rice

2 cups water

2½ cups coconut milk

¼ cup plus 1 tablespoon sugar

2 tablespoons sweetened
   condensed milk

½ teaspoon salt

1. Put the taro root in a medium saucepan and cover with water. Boil for about 15 minutes or until soft. Drain, let cool, and peel. Dice into 1½-inch cubes. Set aside.

2. Put the rice and 2 cups water in a medium saucepan. Cook, uncovered, for about a half hour over medium heat, stirring every 5 minutes or so, as the rice may bubble over as it is cooking. The rice will be completely cooked when its starches have thickened to a sticky texture and just a little bit of water remains.

3. Reduce the heat to a simmer. Add the taro root cubes, 2 cups of the coconut milk, ¼ cup of the sugar, the condensed milk, and salt. Stir thoroughly, then simmer for 10 minutes. Remove from the heat.

4. In a small bowl, blend together the remaining ½ cup coconut milk and 1 tablespoon sugar for the topping.

5. The dessert can be served hot or at room temperature. Spoon into individual bowls and top each serving with a few dollops of the coconut milk and sugar mixture.

[SERVES 4]

BANANA TAPIOCA IN COCONUT MILK
Chè Chuối

Banana che is probably the easiest che to make, and it is also the sweetest. Cooking with tapioca pearls is somewhat tricky, so carefully follow the directions here. The first few times I tried this dish, however, I had to resort to a bailout plan. You can use another fruit or root in this recipe; just make sure it's something that can stand up to the heat, like bananas. Berries and citrus fruits would fall apart in the cooking process.

5 cups water

1 cup medium-size tapioca pearls

5 ripe bananas

3 1/2 cups coconut milk

3 tablespoons sweetened condensed milk

3 tablespoons sugar

1/2 teaspoon salt

1/2 tablespoon fresh lemon or lime juice

2 tablespoons sesame seeds

1/3 cup shredded coconut

1. In a large saucepan, heat the 5 cups of water. When it begins to boil, add the tapioca pearls and stir. Lower the heat to a simmer and cook for about 25 minutes, uncovered.

2. Stir every 5 minutes so the tapioca pearls do not clump together or burn at the bottom of the saucepan. The pearls are finished when they are translucent. (If they're chewy, they're not thoroughly cooked.) When cooked properly, the tapioca pearls should be reconstituted and in a thick, gooey, starchy syrup. If the heat is too hot while cooking, the water will evaporate too quickly and you will find the gooey texture appearing before the pearls are cooked through; add a little more water. If somehow there is more water and the pearls are done without the syrupy texture, then drain off the water in a fine-mesh strainer. This will retain not only the tapioca pearls but also the thick starchy substance necessary for the dessert.

3. Keeping the saucepan at a low simmer, peel the bananas, being sure to remove all banana threads. Cut the bananas in half lengthwise, and then cut into 2-inch slices. Add them immediately to the tapioca pearls, stir, and cook, uncovered, for about 5 minutes.

4. Stir the coconut milk, condensed milk, sugar, salt, and lemon or lime juice into the tapioca until the mixture is well blended. Simmer for another 10 minutes, uncovered.

5. The tapioca can be served hot or at room temperature. Pour it into individual bowls or a large serving bowl. Garnish with the sesame seeds and shredded coconut.

[SERVES 6]

Chè Đậu Trắng

This dessert makes it easy for children to eat their vegetables. Che dishes can be overly sweet, especially when not made at home, and many non-Vietnamese simply describe them as sweet bean soups. Black-eyed peas are more commonly used in glutinous rice che than in other Vietnamese dishes. The final product is a viscous rice and bean mixture. You can substitute black beans or green beans for the black-eyed peas.

³/4 cup dried black-eyed peas, uncooked

³/4 cup glutinous rice

3 cups water

2 cups coconut milk

¹/4 cup plus 1¹/2 tablespoons sugar

¹/2 teaspoon salt

¹/2 tablespoon vanilla extract

1. Put the black-eyed peas in a medium saucepan, cover them with water, and boil for 20 minutes or until soft. Drain and set aside to cool.

2. Put the rice and water in a medium saucepan. Cook, uncovered, for about a half hour over medium heat, stirring every 5 minutes or so, as the rice may bubble over as it is cooking. The rice will be completely cooked when its starches have thickened to a sticky texture and just a little bit of water remains.

3. Add 1¹/4 cups of the coconut milk, ¹/4 cup of the sugar, and the salt to the rice. Blend thoroughly, dissolving the sugar and salt. Then add the cooked black-eyed peas, stir gently, and continue simmering for another 5 minutes (do not mash the beans into the rice mixture). Remove from the heat.

4. For the topping, in a small bowl blend together the remaining ³/4 cup coconut milk, 1¹/2 tablespoons sugar, and the vanilla with a fork or spoon.

5. Serve the che hot or at room temperature in individual bowls. Top each bowl with a few tablespoons of the coconut and sugar topping.

[SERVES 4 TO 6]

The Vietnamese people—long oppressed in their homeland—relish the right to free speech. Little Saigon Radio and Little Saigon TV, as well as several Vietnamese-language newspapers, have their headquarters in Westminster and Garden Grove. Moran Street, right off Bolsa Avenue, is known as the "media street." It's a short street of industrial buildings housing the *Nguoi Viet* newspaper (which has been around since the beginning of Little Saigon), Nguoi Viet Community Center, Vietnamese Arts and Letters Association, *Vien Dong* newspaper, and more. These media sources are broadcast and distributed throughout California, as well as in growing Vietnamese communities in Houston and Dallas. Community-focused but non-Vietnamese language newspapers including *Viet Weekly* and *Asia Week* are also growing in popularity among the English-reading second generation.

Bánh Flan

This easy-to-make dessert has been a household treat since the French first introduced it to the Vietnamese. It seems like every cuisine has some kind of flan or custard variation, but this light and fluffy version is especially similar to the French crème caramel. For a Vietnamese touch, make the dish in a rice bowl or use rock sugar for the caramelization. I have enjoyed making this flan with the zest of mandarin orange or even our beloved lime added to the custard mixture. Keep the flan in the refrigerator right until you serve it. If you remove it from the rice bowls or ramekins too early, it will weep and soften too fast.

1¹/₂ cups sugar

5 large eggs

1¹/₂ cups milk

1 tablespoon vanilla extract

Pinch of salt

1. The flan can be made in the oven or the steamer. If using the oven, preheat it to 325 degrees.

2. In a small saucepan, heat ¹/₂ cup of the sugar over low heat to caramelize the sugar. Keep stirring the sugar to prevent it from burning as it thickens. Cook until the sugar has become a light brown, caramel-colored syrup. Pour the syrup evenly into individual ramekins or china rice bowls.

3. In a medium bowl, beat the eggs, the remaining 1 cup sugar, milk, vanilla extract, and salt until the salt and sugar are dissolved. Pour the mixture through a fine sieve. Next fill the ramekins evenly over the caramel bottoms. Do not allow the custard and caramel to blend together.

4. To cook the flan in the oven, place the ramekins in a deep baking dish or soufflé dish. Fill the dish with hot water until it reaches halfway to the top of the ramekins. Bake in the preheated oven for 35 minutes, or until the center of the flan is firm. Remove the ramekins from the hot water and let cool for 10 minutes.

5. If using a steamer, preheat the steamer over high heat. When the water is hot, place the ramekins in the steamer for 25 to 30 minutes, or until center is firm. Remove the ramekins from the steamer and let them cool for 10 minutes.

6. Place the ramekins in the refrigerator. Keep chilled until the last minute before serving. Turn out the flan onto plates before serving.

[MAKES 6 INDIVIDUAL FLANS]

FRIED BANANAS WITH COCONUT SAUCE
Chuối Chiên

The combination of sweet rice flour and cornstarch gives these fried bananas the perfect golden-brown crisp. Vietnamese desserts don't have too much sugar, so if you have a bit of a sweet tooth, add more sugar to the flour batter, or just serve additional spoonfuls of the creamy coconut dipping sauce. Plantains, when available, are even better than bananas for frying because they're sweeter and meatier. Look for yellow-skinned plantains, not the green ones.

1/2 cup sweet rice flour

1/2 cup cornstarch

1/4 cup sugar

1/3 cup flaked or shredded coconut

1/4 teaspoon salt

1/2 cup vegetable or olive oil for deep-frying

1 1/2 cups coconut milk

2 ripe bananas, but not too mushy

1/2 tablespoon vanilla extract

1/3 cup sweetened condensed milk

1. In a medium bowl, blend together the rice flour, cornstarch, sugar, 1/4 cup of the flaked coconut, and the salt. Transfer the flour mixture to a shallow dish.

2. Pour the oil into a wok or a deep skillet. Heat over high heat until the oil is 350 degrees. You can test the oil by placing a pinch of the rice flour mixture in it; the oil should start frying and sizzling around the flour.

3. Pour 1/2 cup of the coconut milk into a small bowl.

4. Peel bananas and slice into 2 1/2-inch pieces. Set aside.

5. With your hands, dip banana pieces, one at a time, into the coconut milk just enough to give it a light coating. Shake off any excess liquid to prevent the flour from clumping. Lightly roll the banana piece into the flour mixture and completely coat. Place the banana immediately in the hot oil. Repeat with each of the banana pieces.

6. If the oil is 350 degrees, it should take about 3 minutes for each banana piece to fry to a golden brown on each side. Flip them over just once in the hot oil. Remove from the skillet and drain over a rack or set aside on paper towels to soak up excess oil.

7. For coconut sauce, stir together in a small bowl the remaining cup of coconut milk, vanilla extract, and condensed milk. Pour it into small individual dishes for dipping.

8. Serve the fried bananas hot, garnished with the remaining flaked coconut and individual coconut sauce dipping dishes.

[SERVES 2]

FRESH PINEAPPLE AND POMELO WITH CHILI POWDER AND SALT
Trái Thơm Bưởi Với Ớt Màu Muối

Pomelo is the Vietnamese grapefruit that looks like a grapefruit on steroids. When it's ripe, it can be very sweet, a perfect complement for sweet pineapple. The Vietnamese like to salt (and sometimes add chili to) their sweet tropical fruits. Pineapple and pomelo are no different. A little bit of heat from the chili powder and the right amount of salt make for a popular and refreshing snack.

1 large pomelo, peeled

2 cups sliced or diced fresh or canned pineapple

1 tablespoon chili powder

1 tablespoon salt

1. Using a sharp knife, cut between the membranes of the pomelo to release the segments.

2. If using canned pineapple, make sure it is properly drained.

3. Arrange the pineapple pieces and pomelo segments over a large platter. Sprinkle the chili powder and salt evenly over the fruit. Serve immediately or keep in refrigerator until ready.

[SERVES 4]

Don't miss taking an excursion to the tofu "factories" in the area, such as Dong Phuong Tofu. Not quite warehouses, these are special soy sellers that make brick-shape tofu right before your eyes. Not only can you buy fresh tofu, but you'll also find a number of other fresh soy products—like soybean milk, tempeh, or soy nuts—before they are sent out to stores all over Los Angeles and Orange Counties. My favorite thing to buy is a soft, warm tofu dessert (dau hu gung). The consistency is like a custard, served with a hot, sweet ginger sauce.

FRESH AVOCADO SHAKE
Sinh Tô Avocado

Some may shy away from an avocado shake because they cannot imagine avocado served in a fruit drink. I encourage you to take the leap into enjoying the wonder of avocado the way the Vietnamese see and appreciate it. An avocado sinh to (fruit shake) is served in most bakeries and coffeehouses in Little Saigon. It is rich, creamy, sweet, and filling. Condensed sweetened milk is the ingredient of choice, but you can substitute coconut milk and sugar for a different taste.

2 medium avocados, skinned and
   pitted
1$\frac{1}{2}$ cups crushed ice
$\frac{1}{3}$ cup sweetened condensed milk
   (or 1 cup coconut milk and 2
   tablespoons sugar)

In a blender, blend the avocados, ice, and condensed milk. The consistency should be thick, like that of a milk shake. Serve immediately before the avocados turn brown.

[SERVES 2]

FRESH STRAWBERRY SHAKE
Sinh Tô Dâu

The Vietnamese sinh to, or fruit shake, made with coconut milk and condensed milk, is capable of really highlighting the subtle fragrance of the popular strawberry. Though this recipe calls for strawberries, you can easily substitute any fresh fruit—pineapple, bananas, apples, or whatever you like.

2 cups fresh whole strawberries,
   stems removed, washed and
   dried
1 cup crushed ice
$\frac{1}{4}$ cup sweetened condensed milk
$\frac{1}{2}$ cup coconut milk

Put all the ingredients in a blender. Blend until smooth. Pour into glasses and serve immediately.

[SERVES 2]

SALTY LIME SODA
Soda Muối Chanh

This is a subtle and refreshing version of a popular Vietnamese drink known as salty lemonade. In Vietnam it's made with kaffir limes, which are abundant there. But in this country, an ordinary lime will have to suffice. If this beverage is not made with seltzer, it's just limeade.

4 medium limes
½ cup sugar
1 teaspoon salt
8 cups seltzer
Ice

1. In a small bowl or with a juicer, squeeze the limes to extract the juice along with some pulp. Remove the seeds.

2. In a large pitcher, dissolve the sugar and salt in the seltzer. Add the lime juice and ice and serve.

[MAKES 8 CUPS]

Che desserts are sweet desserts sold all over southern Vietnam, but rarely in the North. They normally consist of various combinations of tapioca, dried beans, sweetened coconut milk, fresh fruit, and sugar. Che is served after a meal, but also as a snack or breakfast. Many tourists come to Little Saigon in search of good che. Che Cali is a popular che chain with a number of stores around Little Saigon, and I don't think I have ever seen one without at least a dozen people in line at any given time. Che is quite often sold by street vendors or at larger markets such as ice cream shops. Che is not difficult to make, but finding the balance among the coconut milk, salt, and sugar, and mastering the viscosity and texture of the ingredients are nuances that many appreciate and look for. At a che shop in Little Saigon, you can find many variations, including lotus seeds, tapioca, and even seaweed.

ICED ESPRESSO WITH CONDENSED MILK
Café Sũa Dá

Coffee beans first came to Vietnam during the French occupation of the country. Cafe sua da (pro-nounced cafe soo da) is another example of the Vietnamese taking a foreign food and making it their own. Sweetened condensed milk—the Vietnamese favorite ingredient for sweetening drinks and desserts—is combined here with intensely strong coffee to make a delicious drink. You can get a plastic cup of it in any establishment that sells food—restaurants, delis, bakeries, you name it. You'll see everyone ordering and drinking the beverage throughout the day. At a price of $1.00, this certainly is better priced than any Starbucks blend.

3 tablespoons sweetened condensed milk
½ cup crushed ice
⅓ cup strong hot espresso,
   preferably from slow espresso
   drip

Fill the bottom of a large cup or tall glass with the condensed milk. Add the crushed ice to the glass. Pour the hot espresso over the ice. Stir until everything is blended. Leave the spoon in the glass because as the ice melts, you will need to keep stirring to mix the ingredients together.

[SERVES 1]

GINGER AND JASMINE TEA
Trà Gừng

Ginger tea is a must if you are from Hue or the central region of Vietnam. It's a custom of the region and so easy to make. Boiling the water with the ginger makes the tea more flavorful and aromatic. Try adding fresh ginger slices to other Asian teas like chrysanthemum and green as well.

5 cups water
5 slices peeled fresh ginger
2 tablespoons jasmine tea leaves

Bring the water and ginger slices to a boil in a saucepan or teakettle. Put the jasmine leaves in a teapot. Pour the boiling water and ginger slices into the teapot. Let steep for at least 5 minutes before serving.

[MAKES 5 CUPS]

Appendix A:

INGREDIENTS IN VIETNAMESE CUISINE

The following herbs, vegetables, and fruits are common in Vietnamese dishes. If you are too far away from an Asian grocery store, many large American supermarkets sell a number of these items, and some grocers might even be willing to place an order for you. You can also order many items online through one of the ethnic grocers listed in the next appendix. But if you do have a chance to go to an Asian supermarket, by all means load up on fish sauce, chili paste, fermented shrimp paste, sesame seed oil, coconut milk, coconut soda, spices for pho, and as many varieties of dried noodles as you can find.

Anchovy paste (mắm nêm)**:** Made from fermented anchovies and salt. Add a few teaspoons (or heaping tablespoons!) to nuoc mam (fish sauce) to dilute the paste into pungent dipping sauce. Add a small amount to soup stocks for shellfish flavor.

Anise seeds: See *star anise.*

Annato seeds (hột điều màu)**:** Generally used to give bright reddish orange color to curries and soups and spice rubs for meats. The seeds are usually bled in hot oil for color and then discarded.

Artichoke (ar-ti-chô)**:** Edible thistle brought to Vietnam by the French during their occupation; now grown in Central Vietnam highlands. Most popular when steamed or brewed into a tea.

Asparagus (măng tây)**:** Also introduced by the French. Spears are steamed, sautéed in stir-fries, or added to soups such as sup mang cua. Both white and green asparagus are grown and used.

Avocado (trái bơ)**:** Also introduced by the French in 1940; grows well in Vietnam's tropical climate. Considered a fruit, so mixed into a shake or ice cream, or eaten raw with sugar. Not used in salads or made into guacamole as in Western cooking.

Baby corn (bắp nhỏ)**:** Popular with more Chinese-style dishes, liked for its earthy taste and tiny size. Good in stir-fries, noodle dishes, and canh (consommés).

Bamboo shoots (măng)**:** Best eaten fresh for a sweet crunch. Sold fresh from plastic tubs, but generally soaked in brine immediately after being harvested.

Canned bamboo is most appropriate for soups and stir-fries.

Banana (chuối): Many types in Vietnam; vary in texture and sweetness. Eaten as a snack, but also used grilled, fried, and in various tapioca desserts.

Banana blossom (bắp chuối): Flower of the banana plant; it's popular in salads, salad platters, and as a garnish for noodle soups. The outer layer is tough and needs to be discarded. Soak the white or yellow core in water with lime or lemon juice to avoid discoloration.

Banana leaves (lá chuối): Primarily used for steaming foods, especially fish, as well as wrapping many sticky Vietnamese treats (thus they're called the aluminum foil of the tropics). Adds great aroma to any food. Also used as a garnish and to line plates.

Beans, Asian long (đậu đũa): Vietnamese translation: chopstick beans. Can grow up to 3 feet. Taste and look like green beans, but are young pods of dry black-eyed peas. Appreciated for their crunch. Blanched green beans are a substitute.

Bitter melon (khổ hoa/dưa đắng): Popular gourd melon in South Vietnam with tough and knobby skin and a bitter flavor that is an acquired taste. After being cored and its seeds removed, it's served stuffed or cooked in sauté or a canh (consommé). Quite often served for Tet.

Black pepper (tiêu): Abundant in all Vietnamese dishes; enjoyed for its heat as well as its biting, yet aromatic taste. Introduced to Vietnamese cuisine before the first century. The combination of black pepper, salt, and lime is an extremely popular condiment for fish, shellfish, soups, salads, and stir-fries.

Black tree mushroom (nấm hương): Among the more expensive of Asian mushroom varieties; often served in stir-fries and sautés for its earthy and robust fragrance. Generally purchased in dried form and reconstituted; add liquid from reconstituting to dish you are cooking.

Bok choy (cải bẹ trắng): Member of the cabbage family; very versatile. Most often stir-fried with some oil or oyster or hoisin sauce. The whole plant is edible, but the bottom third of stalks is often discarded.

Broccoli, Chinese (cải làng): Different from Western broccoli because it has flowers and round stem leaves attached to the head. More like Italian rapini than the familiar Western broccoli florets. Western broccoli can be substituted if needed.

Cardamom (bạch đậu khấu, trúc sa): Relative of the ginger plant. The seeds are reddish brown with a warm and aromatic flavor. Very popular in Asian curries. Certain varieties yield a smoky or peppery flavor. Black cardamom is frequently grown in the mountains of Vietnam.

Cellophane noodles (miến)**:** See *noodles, cellophane.*

Cherimoya/custard apple (măng cầu)**:** Green, thin, inedible skin opens into a delicious, milky fruit with a sweet-and-sour taste and wonderful fragrance.

Chili paste (tương ớt)**:** Fine mash of hot red chiles with garlic, salt, and oil. It's a necessary condiment at the Vietnamese table, especially with noodle soups. Not to be confused with chili powder.

Chili powder (ớt màu)**:** Not often used in Vietnamese cuisine because chili paste, Sriracha chili sauce, and fresh Thai bird chiles are preferred. But the color and heat of powder are necessary for bun bo hue noodle soup. The powder is a blend of chili peppers, cumin seeds, garlic, and salt, but Vietnamese like it to include paprika. Try Richin or Sing Kung brands.

Chinese cabbage (cải xanh)**:** Many versions of this. Long outer leaves are light green with white midrib. Napa cabbage is a common version. Great in stir-fries and soups. Do not substitute purple or red cabbage, which tend to bleed when cooked. See also *mustard greens.*

Chinese chives (hoa hẹ)**:** Stiffer and more onion-flavored than the Western variety. Whole stems are enjoyed raw or often used in spring rolls.

Chinese cinnamon/cassia (quế thanh, quế đơn)**:** Derived from the bark of the cassia tree. Much more pungent than ordinary cinnamon and less aromatic and lively. Considered slightly bitter. An essential ingredient in five-spice powder and popular in strong broths such as pho, as well as in braising.

Chinese sausage (lạp xưởng)**:** Dried, sweet sausage usually made of pork. Round, reddish, and popular in stir-fries.

Cilantro (ngò, mùi)**:** Also known as Chinese parsley. Those who enjoy its tangy, citrusy taste add it to broths, wrap it around food, or use it as garnish. See also *long coriander* and *Vietnamese coriander.*

Coconut (dừa)**:** Fruit of the tropical palm tree. Coconut meat is essential to many Vietnamese desserts; it's often dried and sprinkled on top (see *coconut, dried*). Coconut water, the liquid in fresh coconut, is sweet and clear and often used as natural sweetener in tapioca desserts (che) as well as in braising meats, seafood, and poultry. When coconut water is unavailable, a sweet, carbonated coconut soda (Coco Rico) or even 7Up or Sprite can be substituted. See also *coconut milk.*

Coconut, dried (dừa khô)**:** Also known as shredded or flaked coconut. Made from drying out shreds of coconut meat taken from the shell. Most store brands are sweetened and treated with sulfites to keep the flakes white. Natural dried coconut flakes are brown and unsweetened. For desserts, use the sweetened variety. Dried coconut is often dyed and served like candy during holidays. Asian markets sell bags of large, dried coconut flakes.

Coconut milk (nước dừa sữa)**:** Has a creamy milk texture perfect for curries, che, and some batter mixtures. Made by boiling equal amounts of water and shredded, mature coconut flesh until foamy, then straining. Commonly purchased, not homemade. Chaokoh and Mae Ploy brands are recommended; the first is lighter with a hint of sweetness, while Mae Ploy is nice and thick.

Coriander seeds (hột mùi, ngò)**:** Seeds of the cilantro plant with a nutty fragrance that's a combination of lemon or lime and sage. They're a key ingredient in many soups and curries. Sold as seeds (preferred by cooks) or ground. To enhance flavoring, lightly dry-roast the seeds in a skillet before crushing with a mortar and pestle.

Cornstarch (bột bắp)**:** Used as thickening agent in many cooked dishes.

Cucumber (dừa leo)**:** Besides being shredded, julienned, chopped, and thrown into goi and served in salad platters, it can be cooked, becoming velvety and refreshing.

Cumin (ku min)**:** Most common in dried form. Seeds are often crushed with a mortar and pestle to be added to soups, curries, and other skillet-cooked dishes. It has a characteristically strong, musty, and earthy flavor.

Curry paste (tưởng cà-rí)**:** Available ready-made (Mae Ploy is a good brand), which will shorten your cooking time, but many prefer to put together their own spices for curry dishes. All versions have garlic, salt, onion, and chile; they vary in such spices as tamarind, lemongrass, or shrimp paste.

Curry powder (bột cà-rí)**:** Powder does not actually come from curry leaves but from ground roasted cumin and coriander seeds, black pepper, and chiles. Turmeric is also added. The powder is used not just for flavor but also for the yellow coloring of turmeric. Madras is a good brand.

Daikon (củ cải trắng)**:** White radish that looks like a gargantuan carrot; it's often sold in cut pieces. It's used to sweeten soups and broths; also julienned and added to salads for its slightly pungent taste.

Durian (sầu riêng)**:** Grows so large with a thorny shell, it can be mistaken for an armored animal. Husk opens to a sweet, yellow fruit with custardlike consistency. The smell can be unbearable to some. Often made into ice cream, a shake (sinh to), or a fruit drink.

Eggplant, Asian or Japanese (cà tím)**:** Less rotund and bitter than globe eggplant. Commonly salted before being cooked to break down proteins and acids and to sweat out bitterness.

Fish sauce (nước mắm)**:** Fermented, clear brown sauce, found in varying grades. Asian markets often stock more than fifty varieties. Used in virtually every Vietnamese dish.

Five-spice powder (ngủ vị hương)**:** From the Chinese, a powdered combination of fennel seeds, cinnamon, cloves, ginger, and star anise. It can be used as a rub for meats, especially duck and pork.

Galangal (riềng)**:** Similar in look to gingerroot, but more sour and peppery, and pinkish in color. It's used in curries and soups or to season meats and seafood. When served fresh, it's mildly spicy with a refreshing odor. Much spicier in its dried form.

Garlic (tỏi)**:** Often minced and used in sautéing; also pickled to eat with snacks and main dishes. When cooked with ginger, it makes a great complement for many dishes.

Ginger (gừng)**:** Acidic in taste when raw. Peeled roughly and cooked in many dishes for its heat and pungent taste. Because of its fragrance, it's often added to soup stocks or caramelized into syrup.

Guava (ổi)**:** Pear-shaped with edible, green skin and grown from a bush. It's most often enjoyed when unripe and not too sweet, with a bit of salt and Thai bird chile.

Hoisin sauce (tương)**:** From the Chinese, a sweet condiment made from soybean, chili, salt, and sugar. It has a thick, black consistency and is used for cooking and as a dipping sauce, especially with pho.

Jackfruit (mít)**:** Gourdlike fruit that grows quite large with rough texture. The thick skin is broken through to reveal a fruit with a chewy, yellow flesh and strong fragrance. Ripened jackfruit is mixed into beverages and shakes.

Jicama (củ sắn)**:** Sometimes used in sautéed dishes; more commonly julienned and served in salads, banh cuon fillings, and soups. Its crunchy, juicy texture and subtle flavor make it a very popular snack. The brown skin is inedible and needs to be peeled.

Lemongrass (xả/sả)**:** Wonderful fragrance and flavor. Usually diced very fine and then cooked in meat dishes. The outer layers of the stalks must be removed, their ends trimmed, and their layers unraveled. Flatten each layer with a knife and very finely chop it, or diners could feel they are eating shards of metal. Whole stalks, without outer layers, can soak in curries and soups to add a bit of "lemony" zing; remove the stalks before serving. If fresh lemongrass is unavailable, soak dried lemongrass stalks for about 15 to 20 minutes in tepid water after removing the outer layers.

Lime (chấp, chanh xanh)**:** Originates in Southeast Asia. Used in marinades and dipping sauces and on salad platters. Vietnamese enjoy a squeeze of lime over soup.

Longan (nhãn)**:** Similar to lychees in taste and texture, but half the size and much sweeter and juicier. Predominantly found in the Mekong Delta, they have much lighter and thinner skin than lychees.

Long coriander (mùi tàu)**:** Very popular garnish, especially for pho. It's also chopped and used for stir-fries or wrapped around foods. Fragrant, but less pungent than cilantro.

Lotus seeds (hột sen)**:** Popular, fragrant seeds used for che desserts and in beverages. The seeds are purchased in dried form and soaked overnight before use.

Lychee (trái vải)**:** Available fresh or canned. Often served in che desserts and beverages. Peel the dark red, lumpy husk to reveal a fragrant, soft, white-fleshed fruit.

Maggi Seasoning Sauce (Mag-gi)**:** As common to the Vietnamese as soy sauce is to the Chinese; it's kept at every kitchen table with salt and pepper. Made from vegetable proteins. The taste is a cross between dark Chinese soy sauce and Worcestershire sauce. It's added to steamed rice, used as marinade, put in salad dressings—anything requiring some salt. A Swiss product manufactured by Nestlé, it's imported to Vietnam by the French.

Mango (xoài)**:** One of the sweetest and most popular tropical fruits when ripened. It's served in shakes or fruit drinks, and also used unripened in salads.

Mangosteen (măng cụt)**:** Purple-skinned fruit, quite rare in Western countries. The flesh is much like lychee but with a more sweet-and-sour taste. Popular complement to durian.

Mint (bạc hà)**:** Vietnamese mint is rounder than the Western variety and has a hint of spearmint.

Monosodium glutamate/MSG (bột ngọt)**:** Popular in some Asian foods as a "flavor enhancer," but not recommended in this book. It's a product of the fermentation process of molasses and sugar. For some, MSG in foods results in migraines, dizziness, nausea, and more. Best to avoid while its safety remains open for debate.

Mung beans (đậu xanh)**:** Small, cylindrical beans with a bright green skin. Used whole, but the split and hulled version is more common and yellow in color. They do not require presoaking. Cooked beans are often spread over rice flour pastas; packed into a savory, sticky rice mix with meat; or used in che and other sweet desserts.

Mung bean sprouts (gía)**:** The most popular, most common bean sprouts in Vietnamese cuisine. Subtle flavor. Valued for crunch. Generally they're used fresh as a garnish in soups, or in salads or spring rolls (goi cuon). Occasionally steamed when served with hu tieu or more Chinese-style dishes, or even sautéed as a side dish.

Mustard greens (cải tàu)**:** Popular name for the Chinese mustard cabbage. It resembles a head of lettuce, but its leaves are much more fibrous with uneven edges and thick stalks. A popular green in Vietnamese dishes, such as soups and stir-fries. It's so tough that it doesn't wilt quickly. When cooked, the taste becomes milder.

Noodles, cassava (miến, nhỏ = thin): Made from cassava root. Very long, thin threads are cut into smaller pieces when served. The texture is much chewier than rice vermicelli, so it's best served in soup broths or as a stir-fry.

Noodles, cellophane (miến, lớn = thick): Fine, string-like, transparent, and slippery noodles made from green mung bean paste. Similar to cassava noodles (both are called mien), but much thicker. Much firmer than rice noodles. Also called glass noodles.

Noodles, egg (mì): Chinese. Yellow in color, they come flat and wide or thin and curly. When long and extra-thin, they're more popular for soups; the wide are common for stir-fries.

Noodles, rice (bánh phở or bánh hủ tiếu): Made from rice flour and water, these are the most common noodles in Vietnamese cooking. When thin, long, and round, they're called rice vermicelli (bun). (*Bun* is also the name of herb noodle salad, always made from rice vermicelli.) Banh hoi is the thinnest version, resembling fine hair, and is most commonly steamed into banh hoi squares. Two thick rice noodles are bun rieu and bun day. Thin, flat, and wide rice noodles are known as rice sticks, or pho and hu tieu noodles. Though banh pho and banh hu tieu are similar in texture, hu tieu have some tapioca flours that make them a bit tougher than pho noodles. Depending on their thickness, rice noodles are either soaked in hot water or boiled for a minute or two to cook. Transparent when cooked.

Noodles, udon (bánh canh): Not often used in Vietnamese cuisine, udon noodles are most common in banh canh gio heo soup. They're made from wheat flour, salt, and water. Round and much thicker than other noodles, they are white in color and chewy in texture.

Olive oil (dầu ô liu): Now replaces lard and vegetable oil in many Vietnamese dishes, making foods lighter and healthier. Recommended for any recipe in this book where oil is called for.

Onion (hành): Essential in all cooked Vietnamese dishes and enjoyed equally in raw form.

Oyster sauce (dầu hào): Introduced by the Chinese, this thick, black sauce made from ground oysters, salt, flour, sugar, and water has the consistency of ketchup. It's used most often in stir-fries and sautés, often to add a sweet and umami flavor.

Palm sugar (đường thẻ): Made from boiled-down sugar from the sap of palm tree flowers. Not as sweet as sugarcane, it's preferred in savory dishes such as soups, dipping sauces, and curries. It has caramel and molasses flavor, and can be used instead of granulated sugar in recipes.

Papaya (đu đủ): When ripened, this gourd fruit is popular as a snack. When green and unripened, its hard flesh is shredded into a tangy salad. It can be pickled and served with salty dishes.

Peanuts (đậu phộng): The Vietnamese enjoy boiled peanuts as a snack. They're often crushed and served as a final touch in salad and beef dishes. Peanut oil, when available, is popular for frying, but more expensive than other oils.

Peas, green (đậu): Valued for their color and texture, peas are added to fried rice and curries for a lift.

Peppermint (bạc hà, rau thơm): Not to be confused with Vietnamese mint, this menthol plant is more popular as a garnish and on a salad platter.

Perilla (lá tía tô): Used as garnish for noodle soups and on salad platters for wrapping around food. The purple variety is more common in Vietnamese food than the green, and appreciated for its complex and subtle flavor. The leaves are fragrant and resemble mint in shape; they're green on one side and reddish purple on the other. The taste and aroma combine hints of cinnamon, licorice, and anise.

Persimmon (trái hồng): A reddish orange seasonal fruit. Soft and creamy when ripened, but also popular as hard fruit. It makes a great spiced fruit, with a cinnamon fragrance.

Pineapple (trái thơm): Most common in South Vietnam; served as a snack with some salt and a little bit of chile. Pineapple juice (nuoc thom, meaning "perfumed liquid") is essential in canh chua (sweet-and-sour fish soup) and other seafood broths.

Pomelo (bưởi): *Giant* version of the grapefruit. The skin is extremely thick, but the fruit is much sweeter and less acidic than a typical grapefruit. Regarded as a sign of good luck, it often adorns altars and shrines in homes, businesses, and Buddhist temples. Like other sweet fruits, it's enjoyed with a sprinkle of salt and eaten as a snack.

"Pork patty" (chả lụa): Best described as lean pork cold cut, like a Vietnamese bologna. Found in almost every Vietnamese fridge. Rarely homemade. Processed meat is bundled tightly with banana leaves, and then boiled or steamed. It's made into a sandwich, eaten as a snack, or sliced thin and served over bun.

Potato starch (bột khoai): Popular as glue or thickener for many meat and seafood dishes in which food is cooked in its juices. It provides a nice crunch to the items it coats when lightly fried.

Rambutan (chôm chôm): Found only in the tropics. The rind is bright red with sparse red hairs. Under its thick skin, the fruit is similar to the lychee, to which it is related.

Rice (gạo = uncooked; cơm = cooked): Steamed, white jasmine rice is served with almost every meal. Necessary with salty Vietnamese dishes.

Rice, glutinous (bột nếp = uncooked; xôi = cooked): Also known as sushi rice or sticky rice, this short-grain rice with a sticky, starchy consistency serves as the base for many creamy rice puddings. It's most common in che, but also found in other sweet treats.

Rice flour (bột gạo)**:** The only flour the Vietnamese know. It's used for frying foods, making crepes and breads, and more.

Rice noodles: See *noodles, rice.*

Rice paddy flower (ngò ôm, rau ngổ)**:** Soft herb with a citrus fragrance. Popular in fish-based soups like canh chua or bun rieu. Also good in salads.

Rice paper (bánh tráng)**:** Most commonly used for spring rolls; it's also eaten with grilled meats and fish and salad platters, similar to a tortilla. Complicated to make. Sold dry in packages, it's paper-thin and can easily crack. Before use, it must be briefly soaked in warm water to become pliable. If it's too hard, it will crack; too soft and it won't hold anything together.

Rice vinegar (giấm)**:** There are three types—red, black, and white. The black and red are much sweeter but more popular in Chinese cooking than Vietnamese. The red is not often used in Vietnamese cooking but is found as a table condiment. White rice vinegar is used in cooking and to prepare salad dressings.

Rock sugar (đường phèn)**:** Crystallized form of sugar mainly used for stocks like pho or hu tieu. Made from white sugar, brown sugar, and honey, it's richer in taste but more subtle and mellow than granulated sugar. Gives soup stocks a nice sheen. Crush with a hammer or in a mortar and pestle to break apart.

Scallions (hành xanh)**:** Also known as green onions. Immature onions with mild flavor, and more popular in Vietnamese cuisine. They're often chopped and eaten raw or cooked in sautés or stir-fries.

Sesame seeds (mè)**:** Most often used as garnish for desserts and some family-style main dishes. Sesame seed oil is extracted from seeds and used for salad dressings, sautéing, and frying.

Shallots (hành hương)**:** The offspring of spring onion and garlic parents, shallots are used as much as yellow onions in Vietnamese sautés, stir-fries, and stocks. They're often fried and used as a garnish.

Shallots, pickled (củ kiệu chua)**:** Often purchased at the grocery store in a simple jar. To make at home, pickle young, spring bulbs with rice vinegar, salt, and sugar. Great contrast to salty dishes and served with most salad platters and plates of garnishes.

Shrimp, dried (tom khô)**:** Special shrimp specifically harvested for drying and curing. Sold in packages. Usually reconstituted and added to stir-fries or thrown directly into the beginnings of a stock or broth. If reconstituted, save the liquid that accumulates and add it to sauces, stir-fries, or soups. It can be finely chopped when dry and used as a topping over rice dishes, soups, and goi.

Shrimp paste (mắm ruốc)**:** Sold as pink- or brown-colored fermented paste in Asian markets. Packed with sodium and the taste of shellfish. Just a little bit should be added to soups like bun rieu or to sautéed seafood.

Soybeans (đậu nành)**:** The basis for many products, including soy milk, tofu, and bean curd. They're also good in some desserts, or can be boiled and used for sticky treats wrapped with banana leaves. Delicious dried as a snack.

Soy sauce (nước tương)**:** Less popular in Vietnamese cuisine than fish sauce (nuoc mam). The best liked are those that are thick and dark, with the pungent flavor of mushrooms.

Sriracha chili sauce (tương ớt Sriracha)**:** A smooth, almost liquid chili sauce sold in convenient squeeze bottles. Made from ripe red chiles and garlic, it's a popular condiment at every noodle house, and often added to soups, sauces, marinades. Not as flavorful or dense as chili paste, but equal in heat.

Star anise (hồi hương)**:** Aromatic, with a sweet taste similar to fennel or licorice. Very popular in soups, and fundamental to pho. Its shape is an eight-pointed star. The seeds and pods are used for stocks and sometimes sautés but must be removed before serving.

Star fruit (khế)**:** Shiny-skinned fruit with five points, usually cut to highlight its star shape. It's available in different colors and known for its sweet but slightly tart taste.

Straw mushrooms (nấm rơm)**:** Tiny yellowish brown mushrooms with umbrella-shaped caps. They're generally used from the can, in which they are soaked in brine. Their slightly milky and pungent flavor is popular in stir-fries and soups.

Sweet rice flour (bột nếp)**:** Also called glutinous rice flour. Most common in che desserts and other sweet treats.

Tamarind (me)**:** Sweet-and-sour fruit inside a dry, brown casing; when fully ripe, it's often eaten raw as a snack. Like lemon, tamarind gives an acidic or tart taste to food. The pulp of tender, immature, very sour pods is boiled and ground into a paste that's often sautéed with meat and shellfish dishes. Popular in canh (consommé).

Tapioca beads or pearls (bột báng)**:** Necessary for many Vietnamese desserts such as che. When cooked, they expand and form a thick starchy syrup. Also used in soups.

Tapioca flour (bột năng)**:** Derived from cassava root. Used as thickener like cornstarch, it gives a nice sheen to prepared dishes.

Taro root (khoai môn)**:** A starchy, tuberous vegetable similar to the potato in taste and use, but starchier and stickier in texture. Most common in desserts and tapiocas. The hairy brown skin must be removed; boil first. The center of the root has concentric circles with a bit of purplish coloring.

Taro stem (bạc hà)**:** There are many varieties of taro, but only the stems of the *Colocasia gigantean* are eaten. Not related to stems of taro root. Sliced stems, which are porous, are used in soups, holding flavorful stock like a sponge. They're also great in salads for their delicate flavor and crisp texture.

Thai basil (rau quế)**:** Important herb of salad platters, often wrapped around food. It's also cooked with chicken and seafood dishes, or thrown into soups. More pungent and less sweet than Italian basil.

Thai bird chile (ớt)**:** The most popular—and often only—chile pepper in Vietnamese cuisine, used for extra heat in dishes. The Vietnamese use red and green Thai birds; green is much hotter than red. Chiles have the most heat intensity when used fresh; the seeds should be consumed, never discarded. Serrano peppers or cayenne can be substituted.

Tofu or bean curd (đậu hủ)**:** Made from dried soybeans that are soaked in water and then boiled and processed. Loaded with protein and nutrients, tofu is important in turning meat-based foods into vegetarian ones. Best in sautés, soups, or deep-fried dishes. Firm tofu is a bit chewier and more substantial and will withstand tossing in a stir-fry. Soft tofu will fall apart when sautéed.

Tree ear mushrooms (nấm mèo)**:** Also known as wood ear mushrooms, these are popular for their chewy texture more than their bland flavor. This texture enhances stir-fries, soups, and meat-filled foods such as crepes and fried egg rolls. The smaller, the better. Reconstitute in boiling water. One tablespoon of dried mushrooms becomes 1/3 cup soaked. Squeeze off the excess liquid and add it to a savory stock.

Turmeric (bột nghệ khô)**:** A relative of ginger, most often used in powdered form. Added to food for yellow color and slightly bitter taste. An important ingredient of curries and fish dishes.

Vietnamese coriander (rau răm)**:** The most popular herb among the South Vietnamese, it's redolent of coriander, but with a more lemony scent and taste. Wrap pho meat and seafood with it. Large heaps are chopped and thrown over cooked dishes.

Water spinach (râu muống)**:** A unique spinach grown in marshes and rice fields. Considered Vietnam's official vegetable, it's cherished for its bitter and spinachlike flavor. In some places, Vietnamese Americans have been banned from growing it, because its extensive root system has spread into sewers and drainage systems. When cooked, the leaves have a creamy texture like that of cooked spinach. It melds well with garlic and fish sauce and is common in soups, stir-fries, and salads.

Winter melon (bầu)**:** Light green and oblong in shape, this is actually a squash with a mild, sweet taste popular in soups and stir-fries. It's good at absorbing the flavors of ingredients it is cooked with.

Appendix B:

RESOURCES AND LINKS

FOOD WEB SITES AND BOOKS

www.noodlepie.com
An excellent blog by a British expat, eating his way through Vietnam.

www.wokme.com/ingredients/vietnamese.htm
An in-depth look at Vietnamese ingredients.

www.chowhound.com
This forum can help you find Vietnamese food in your local area.

www.professorsalt.com
"Professor Salt" highlights the ins and outs of eating in Little Saigon, from the nonlocal, non-Vietnamese perspective.

www.vietworldkitchen.com
A great Web site on Vietnamese cooking.

Communion by Kim Fay
Fay writes on eating, shopping, and traveling off the beaten path in Vietnam and Southeast Asia with contributions from writers who work, live, and eat in Asia.

Lonely Planet World Foods of Vietnam by Richard Sterling
A great summary and index on the foods and dining culture of Vietnam.

ONLINE ETHNIC GROCERS

There are plenty of ethnic food Web sites to choose from, but some of them are ridiculously overpriced. These sites below charge reasonable prices for their fare:
www.asianfoodgrocer.com
www.ethnicgrocer.com
www.grocerythai.com
www.pacificrimgourmet.com
www.templeofthai.com

LITTLE SAIGON GROCERS

Asian grocers are popping up all over the country. You don't need to find a specifically Vietnamese grocery store; a nearby Thai or Chinese grocer will provide you with the ingredients and herbs you need. Just check your local phone book or business directory for contact information. Still, Vietnamese grocers are unique. Here are some popular stores to visit in Little Saigon:

A Chau Supermarket
16042 Magnolia Street
Fountain Valley, CA 92708

Ben Thanh Supermarket
9166 Bolsa Avenue
Westminster, CA 92683

Bolsa Supermarket
9550 Bolsa Avenue
Westminster, CA 92683

T&K Market
9681 Bolsa Avenue
Westminster, CA 92683

www.99ranch.com
This chain is popular throughout Southern California.

VIETNAMESE CULTURE AND MEDIA

http://nguoi-viet.com/
Nguoi Viet newspaper, Vietnamese version.

http://nguoi-viet.com/nv2_default.asp
Nguoi Viet newspaper, English version.

www.lib.uci.edu/libraries/collections/sea/seaexhibit/index.html
The University of California–Irvine's Southeast Asian Archive.

www.littlesaigonradio.com
Little Saigon Radio.

http://65.45.193.26:8026/cms/acct/vietweekly/main/
Viet Weekly.

http://nguoi-viet.com/idirectory/businessdetail.asp?Biz_ID=145
Business directory.

The Vietnam War Memorial in Westminster is the centerpiece of the Sid Goldstein Freedom Park. A marble fountain flanks one side of a 15-foot, three-ton bronze statue, while flags of the former South Vietnam and the United States, a constantly burning torch, and a memorial urn are on the other side. The statue, which depicts an American soldier and a South Vietnamese soldier together in combat, was dedicated on April 27, 2003, just three days before the twenty-eighth anniversary of the fall of Saigon. It represents the alliance and friendships between the South Vietnamese and the United States during the Vietnam War and commemorates and honors the 58,000 American and 300,000 South Vietnamese casualties of that war. The people of Little Saigon raised $500,000 themselves before city officials approved the plans for the memorial. These Vietnamese-American refugees and survivors of the reeducation camps have so much love for the memorial that visiting it, praying before it, taking pictures of it, and participating in its maintenance serve as a proud patriotic duty. Many visit here from the community or beyond to place incense in the urn and pray for America and for peace.

VIETNAMESE ORGANIZATIONS

www.vps.org/
Vietnamese Professional Society.

www.vncoc.org/
Vietnamese Community of Orange County.

www.vietfilmfest.com
Vietnamese-American Film Festival, Little Saigon.

www.bpsos.org/
Boat People S.O.S.

THE VIETNAMESE EXPERIENCE

Lost Years: My 1,632 Days in Vietnamese Reeducation Camps by Tran Tri Vu.

Prisoner of the Word: A Memoir of the Vietnamese Reeducation Camps by Le Huu Tri.

Saigon, USA
A documentary on the political side of Little Saigon by Lindsey Jang and Robert C. Winn.

LITTLE SAIGON POINTS OF INTEREST AND ATTRACTIONS

Chùa Quan Âm (temple)
Vietnamese Pure Land
10510 Chapman Avenue, #400
Garden Grove, CA 92844

Chùa Huệ Quang (temple)
4918 West Westminster Avenue
Santa Ana, CA 92703

Vietnam War Memorial
All-American Way
Westminster, CA 92683

Asian Garden Mall
9200 Bolsa Avenue
Westminster, CA 92683

Thư Viện Việtnam, Vietnam Library
14291 Euclid Street, D109
Garden Grove, CA 92843
www.thuvienvietnam.com

GENERAL TOURISM INFORMATION

www.citysearch.com
www.ocregister.com
www.ocregister.com/show/saigon
www.ocweekly.com

Appendix C:

SAMPLE MENUS

BREAKFAST

Any single dish will work:
- Beef Pho
- Rice Noodle Soup in Pork Broth
- Crab and Pork Hock Soup with Udon Noodles
- Spiced Beef Stew with fresh baguettes
- Chicken Rice Porridge with Lemongrass and Ginger

SIMPLE ONE-DISH LUNCHES

Choose any single dish:
- Herb Noodle Salad, anything grilled as a topping— shrimp, beef, pork
- Noodle soups (any)
- Chicken Rice Porridge with Lemongrass and Ginger
- Chicken Curry with Potatoes and Peas
- Spiced Beef Stew
- Traditional Vietnamese Spring Rolls and Spicy Beef Salad with Thai Basil and Lemongrass
- Crispy Coconut and Turmeric Crepes

DINNERS

Steamed Tilapia with Ginger, Scallions, and Onions
Warm "Shaking Beef" Salad with Watercress and Tomatoes
Fried Spring Rolls with Ground Pork, Fresh Crab, and Tree Ear Mushrooms
Steamed Jasmine Rice and Salad Platter

Winter Melon and Shrimp Soup
Pork Braised in Caramel Sauce
Whole Salted Fish with Lemongrass and Chili Paste
Steamed Jasmine Rice and Salad Platter

Mustard Greens with Shrimp Tamarind Soup
Grilled Beef Slices with Chile, Lemongrass, and Honey
Salted Short Ribs in a Clay Pot
Steamed Jasmine Rice and Salad Platter

Cabbage Soup with Ground Pork and Shrimp
Chicken Braised in Ginger and Coconut
Hanoi-style Fried Fish with Turmeric and Dill
Steamed Jasmine Rice and Salad Platter

Sweet-and-Sour Catfish Soup in Pineapple Broth
Grilled Pork Chops with Herb Noodle Salad
Rice Flour Crepes with Mushrooms and Ground Pork
Catfish Braised in Caramel Sauce
Steamed Jasmine Rice and Salad Platter

SPECIAL DIETS

Low Carb

Pan-fried Tofu and Broccoli with Lemongrass
   and Chile
Snow Peas and Shrimp Sautéed in Garlic and
   Oyster Sauce
Grilled Beef with Lemongrass, Garlic, and Chili Paste
Five-spiced Fried Chicken

Vegetarian

Braised Eggplant and Tofu in Caramel Sauce
Vegetarian Sweet-and-Sour Soup
Cabbage Salad with Banana Blossoms
Steamed Jasmine Rice and Salad Platter
Herb Noodle Salad
Winter Melon and Shrimp Soup (omit the shrimp)
Traditional Vietnamese Spring Rolls (substitute
   cucumber for the pork and shrimp)
Vegetarian Fried Rice

PARTIES AND FEASTS

Appetizer Party

Vietnamese do not have appetizer parties, but if you must, you must! Note that you may want to cut these recipes in half to prepare smaller, appetizer-size batches.

Shrimp Brochettes
Fried Spring Rolls with Ground Pork, Fresh Crab,
   and Tree Ear Mushrooms
Traditional Vietnamese Spring Rolls with Pork,
   Shrimp, and Mint Leaves
Fried Squid in Rice Flour Batter
Grilled Shrimp with Garlic, Lemongrass, and
   Chili Paste
Fried Shrimp in Turmeric and Garlic Batter

Produce Party

Green Papaya Salad witih Shrimp
Vegetables and Tofu Sautéed in Oyster Sauce
Vietnamese Water Spinach Sautéed with Garlic
Herb Noodle Salad
Steamed Jasmine Rice

Seafood Party

Fresh Crab Sautéed in Salt and Pepper
Fried Shrimp with Shrimp Paste, Lemongrass,
   and Chili Paste
Mussels Sautéed with Chiles and Thai Basil
Whole Salted Fish with Lemongrass and Chili Paste
Steamed Jasmine Rice and Salad Platter

Family Feast for a Special Occasion

Mussels Sautéed with Chiles and Thai Basil

Drunken Crab

Five-spiced Fried Chicken (substitute duck)

Asparagus and Crab Soup

Beef Tenderloin Cured with Lime Juice and Onions

Traditional Fried Rice

Family Feast with Comfort Foods

Crispy Coconut and Turmeric Crepes

Traditional Shredded Chicken and Cabbage Salad

Chicken Curry with baguettes

Traditional Vietnamese Spring Rolls with Pork,
    Shrimp, and Mint Leaves

Appendix D:

METRIC CONVERSION TABLES
APPROXIMATE U.S.–METRIC EQUIVALENTS

LIQUID INGREDIENTS

U.S. MEASURES	METRIC	U.S. MEASURES	METRIC
1/4 TSP.	1.23 ML	2 TBSP.	29.57 ML
1/2 TSP.	2.36 ML	3 TBSP.	44.36 ML
3/4 TSP.	3.70 ML	1/4 CUP	59.15 ML
1 TSP.	4.93 ML	1/2 CUP	118.30 ML
1 1/4 TSP.	6.16 ML	1 CUP	236.59 ML
1 1/2 TSP.	7.39 ML	2 CUPS OR 1 PT.	473.18 ML
1 3/4 TSP.	8.63 ML	3 CUPS	709.77 ML
2 TSP.	9.86 ML	4 CUPS OR 1 QT.	946.36 ML
1 TBSP.	14.79 ML	4 QTS. OR 1 GAL.	3.79 LT

DRY INGREDIENTS

U.S. MEASURES		METRIC	U.S. MEASURES	METRIC
17 3/5 OZ.	1 LIVRE	500 G	2 OZ.	60 (56.6) G
16 OZ.	1 LB.	454 G	1 3/4 OZ.	50 G
8 7/8 OZ.		250 G	1 OZ.	30 (28.3) G
5 1/4 OZ.		150 G	7/8 OZ.	25 G
4 1/2 OZ.		125 G	3/4 OZ.	21 (21.3) G
4 OZ.		115 (113.2) G	1/2 OZ.	15 (14.2) G
3 1/2 OZ.		100 G	1/4 OZ.	7 (7.1) G
3 OZ.		85 (84.9) G	1/8 OZ.	3 1/2 (3.5) G
2 4/5 OZ.		80 G	1/16 OZ.	2 (1.8) G

Index

About the Author

Ann Le was born in Minneapolis, Minnesota, after her family fled Vietnam as boat people three days before the fall of Saigon in April 1975. The Le family then moved to Southern California, where they were among the first few Vietnamese immigrants to settle and work in Little Saigon. Ann grew up cooking and eating at home with her grandparents, as well as all over Little Saigon. And she has watched the community evolve into the culinary tourist destination it is today.

She has traveled and eaten all over the world, spending months in Asia as well as living in Europe, New York, and San Francisco. Ann believes the finest cuisine belongs to the Vietnamese people, a cuisine with recipes that are never written down, but ingrained in memory. Inspired by the need to share the wealth of Vietnamese cuisine, and for fear of losing recipes passed only through oral history, Ann offers this proud history of a remarkable community and opens the kitchen door to authentic Vietnamese dishes.

About the Photographer

Julie Fay Ashborn has several favorite photo subjects (retro motel signs, Paris, her children), but Vietnam and its culture is her specialty. She has traveled extensively through Southeast Asia and her photographs appear in the books *To Asia with Love, To Vietnam with Love,* and *Communion: A Culinary Journey Through Vietnam.* She was raised in the Pacific Northwest, lived in London, and now resides in Los Angeles with her husband, daughter, and son.